LOST LANES

36 GLORIOUS BIKE RIDES
IN CENTRAL ENGLAND

JACK THURSTON

LOST LANES

CONTENTS

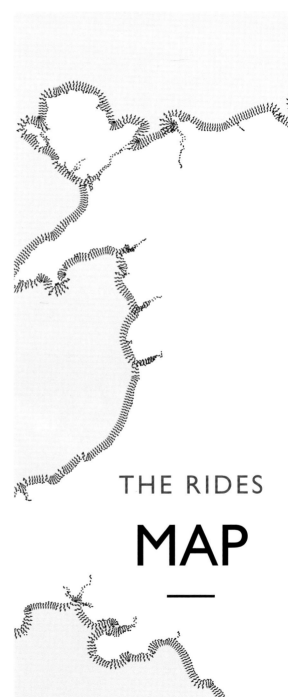

THE RIDES

MAP

—

HOPE

BUXTON

MACCLESFIELD

CHESTERFIELD

WORKSOP

LOUTH

LINCOLN

2

7

1

4

3

28

27

30

STOKE

DENSTONE

ASHBOURNE

DERBY

NOTTINGHAM

6

5

WHITCHURCH

8

UTTOXETER

STAFFORD

LOUGHBOROUGH

MELTON
MOWBRAY

OAKHAM

SHREWSBURY

21

22

LICHFIELD

LEICESTER

26

25

24

WOLVERHAMPTON

9

11

18

BRIDGNORTH

BIRMINGHAM

10

STOURPORT

COVENTRY

LUDLOW

WARWICK

23

12

19

20

WORCESTER

STRATFORD

NORTHAMPTON

13

MALVERN

EVESHAM

MORETON-IN-MARSH

LEDBURY

14

17

GLOUCESTER

15

COLEFORD

16

CIRENCESTER

THE RIDES AT A GLANCE

No.	NAME	COUNTY	START / END	TRAIN STATION	DIRECTIONS & GPX
1	Peak Pleasure	Peak District	Buxton	Buxton	lostlanes.co.uk/01pp
2	Hope Springs Eternal	Peak District	Hope	Hope	lostlanes.co.uk/02hs
3	Super Off Peak	Peak District	Chesterfield	Chesterfield	lostlanes.co.uk/03op
4	Happy Trails	Peak District	Cromford	Cromford	lostlanes.co.uk/04ht
5	Manifold Destiny	Peak District	Ashbourne	Uttoxeter (12 miles from start)	lostlanes.co.uk/05md
6	Staffordshire Rollercoaster	Peak District	Denstone	Uttoxeter (7 miles from start)	lostlanes.co.uk/06sr
7	Natural High	Peak District	Macclesfield	Macclesfield	lostlanes.co.uk/07nh
8	About Time	Shropshire & Worcestershire	Whitchurch	Whitchurch	lostlanes.co.uk/08at
9	Shropshire Thrills	Shropshire & Worcestershire	Shrewsbury	Shrewsbury	lostlanes.co.uk/09st
10	Over the Edge	Shropshire & Worcestershire	Ludlow	Ludlow	lostlanes.co.uk/10oe
11	Take it to the Bridge	Shropshire & Worcestershire	Bridgnorth	Wellington (2 miles from route)	lostlanes.co.uk/11tb
12	Severn Up	Shropshire & Worcestershire	Worcester	Worcester	lostlanes.co.uk/12su
13	I Hear A Symphony	Shropshire & Worcestershire	Ledbury	Ledbury	lostlanes.co.uk/13hs
14	Roads Less Travelled	Gloucestershire	Ledbury	Ledbury	lostlanes.co.uk/14rt
15	Freedom of the Forest	Gloucestershire	Parkend	Lydney (4 miles from start)	lostlanes.co.uk/15ft
16	At the Crossroads	Gloucestershire	Kemble	Kemble	lostlanes.co.uk/16ac
17	This Charming Land	Gloucestershire	Moreton-in-Marsh	Moreton-in-Marsh	lostlanes.co.uk/17tc
18	Canal City	Heart of England	Birmingham	Birmingham	lostlanes.co.uk/18cc
19	Escape Velocity	Heart of England	Birmingham / Warwick	Birmingham	lostlanes.co.uk/19ev
20	A Warwickshire Wander	Heart of England	Leamington Spa	Leamington Spa	lostlanes.co.uk/20ww
21	Cut to the Chase	Heart of England	Lichfield	Lichfield	lostlanes.co.uk/21ct
22	Greenwood, Gravel and Grit	Heart of England	Loughborough	Loughborough	lostlanes.co.uk/22gg
23	To the Manor Born	Heart of England	Northampton	Northampton	lostlanes.co.uk/23mb
24	Small is Beautiful	East Midlands	Oakham	Oakham	lostlanes.co.uk/24sb
25	Higher Ground	East Midlands	Melton Mowbray	Melton Mowbray	lostlanes.co.uk/25hg
26	The Fat of the Land	East Midlands	Melton Mowbray	Melton Mowbray	lostlanes.co.uk/26tf
27	Towers of Power	East Midlands	Newark	Newark	lostlanes.co.uk/27tp
28	The Way through the Woods	East Midlands	Creswell	Creswell	lostlanes.co.uk/28ww
29	Wolds Apart	East Midlands	Lincoln	Lincoln	lostlanes.co.uk/29wa
30	Out to Lunch	East Midlands	Louth	Market Rasen (3 miles from route)	lostlanes.co.uk/30ol

MILES	KM	ASCENT(m)	TERRAIN	GRADE
35	56	904	Mostly lanes with 7 miles on good gravel tracks	Moderate
28	45	764	Lanes with two short off-road sections (1.5 miles total), plus the Mam Tor 'broken road'	Moderate
37	60	793	Mostly lanes, with a 4 mile section of gravel rail-trail	Moderate
41	67	936	Two thirds lanes, one third gravel tracks and unsurfaced byways	Moderate to Challenging
32	52	783	Lanes and tarmac cycleways, with a couple of short sections of unsurfaced byway. One short section of A-road (with footway)	Moderate
31	49	757	Lanes and 11 miles of unsurfaced canal towpath, forest track and rail-trail	Moderate
44	70	1412	Lanes and a short section of traffic-free cycleway	Very challenging
43	69	448	Lanes and 2 miles of unsurfaced canal towpath and rural byway	Easy
44	71	1085	Lanes, 4 miles of good gravel tracks, some urban roads and a very short section of farm byway	Very challenging
49	79	995	Lanes and a few very short sections on A and B roads	Challenging
41	67	992	Lanes and 6 miles of unsurfaced rail-trail	Moderate to Challenging
42	67	682	Lanes and three short unsurfaced sections of canal towpath, bridleway and byway	Moderate
37	60	872	Lanes, quiet B-roads and an optional gravel climb up to the Worcestershire Beacon	Moderate
40	64	866	Lanes and a 1.5 mile section of mostly rideable woodland bridleway	Moderate
38	61	895	Lanes and 12 miles of unsurfaced forest tracks	Challenging
48	77	872	Lanes and a couple of very short sections on A-roads	Moderate
46	74	929	Lanes and 3 miles of good gravel tracks	Challenging
25	40	349	Canal towpath, traffic-free cycleways and quiet roads	Easy
46	74	533	Lanes and traffic-free urban cycleways	Moderate
44	71	532	Lanes and two shortish sections of canal towpath and bridleway	Moderate
45	72	627	Lanes and 10 miles of unpaved towpath and gravel tracks	Moderate to Challenging
45	72	645	Lanes, cycleways, and 15 miles of unpaved tracks, a few of which are rough and can be muddy when wet	Challenging
48	77	678	Lanes, some urban roads and 7 miles of unpaved cycleways and byways	Moderate
51	82	751	Mostly lanes with 9 miles of unpaved lakeside and forest tracks	Moderate to Challenging
34	55	710	Lanes and 2 miles of unpaved rural byways	Moderate
46	74	553	Lanes and 6 miles of unpaved canal towpath and bridleways	Easy
60	97	394	Lanes and 7 miles of good gravel cycleways and byways	Moderate
39	63	526	Half lanes and half unpaved forest tracks and bridleways, with a few rougher sections that can get muddy after rain	Challenging
60	96	625	Lanes, B-roads, traffic-free cycleways, and a 1.5 mile section of unpaved bridleway	Moderate
43	70	593	Lanes and 1.5 miles of unpaved woodland track	Easy

IN SEARCH OF

LOST LANES

—

Britain has a quarter of a million miles of paved roads – about the same distance as from the Earth to the Moon. A third of the network are 'unclassified' rural roads. For *unclassified* you might as well say overlooked and ignored — at least by drivers looking for the quickest route from A to B. This network of quiet country lanes is perfect for exploring the nooks and corners of the British countryside, and the bicycle is the perfect vehicle.

Only a bicycle guarantees total immersion in your surroundings. You not only see the world around you; you hear it, smell it and feel it in your legs and your lungs. To ride a bike is to travel at a pace that is perfectly in tune with the changing character of the landscape. As well as being the most energy-efficient vehicle ever invented, the bicycle is also silent, nimble and pollution-free. It gives you a sense of freedom and self-reliance and a feeling of treading lightly on the land. While a car is always a blot on the landscape, a bicycle adds a touch of beauty to any scene.

Travelling by bicycle you'll soon discover that lost lanes are not just routes between places, they are places in and of themselves. Each one has its own history, character and atmosphere. A lane may bowl you over with breathtaking views, or its allure may be more subtle and ephemeral. While no two lost lanes are entirely alike, there are some definite types that are worth looking out for. It is an odd quirk of human psychology that as soon as we identify something, and give a name to it, then suddenly we start finding it everywhere we look. With this intention in mind, I present my typology of lost lanes.

The holloway is an iconic subspecies of lost lane. Worn over many centuries, holloways are lanes that have sunk beneath the level of the sur-

rounding land. Shady dells lined by exposed tree roots with freakish, gnarled limbs that threaten to reach out and grab, they are places of real enchantment. On a fine summer's day, an arching canopy of leaves glitters with dappled sunlight, in a violent storm the trees shake and sway in the wind. On rare misty mornings, holloways have an architectural quality as shafts of light break through the canopy and pool among the mosses and ferns.

The ridgeway is the polar opposite of the holloway, with an entirely different atmosphere and appeal. While a holloway draws you deeper into the landscape, the ridgeway lifts you up above it. Ridgeways are the original long-distance highways and some date back many thousands of years. They follow the crest of hills over high ground, keeping wayfarers from getting bogged down on the valley floor, safe from bandits and outlaws. Today, these lofty routes delight the traveller with big skies and views to distant horizons. Riding a ridgeway is always exhilarating and comes with a satisfying sense of being above the fray.

The balcony road — a route that traces a single contour around a hillside — is a close relative of the ridgeway, and offers the same elevated vantage point over the surrounding land. In their purest Alpine form, balcony roads are precarious routes hewn into sheer rock faces, with tunnels, cuttings and elaborate support structures. In the gentler terrain of the English countryside they are not quite so perilous, but a balcony road is still thrilling to ride, with a new vista around every bend.

While holloways, ridgeways and balcony roads depend on a very specific situation in the landscape, there is another kind of lost lane that can be created simply by installing a gate at each end of a farm lane. The gates are there are to stop livestock from

wandering, but they do an equally good job of deterring the vast majority of motorists. This makes them havens for cycling. Close relatives of the gated road are those little-used lanes with a thick sward of grass up the middle. It may have grown through of lack of use, or because the centre section of the lane was never tarred in the first place.

Taking grass-up-the-middle to the next level are the lanes which do without a tarmac surface altogether. "Green lane" is a catch-all term that covers a wide variety of unsurfaced ways that includes farm tracks, byways, bridleways and boundary roads. Most are medieval but a handful are even older: unmodernised sections of Roman roads and prehistoric trackways. Cycling these rustic byways is a way of experiencing the slow pace and unpredictability of travel in a bygone time (the word 'travel' derives from *travail* denoting a painful or laborious effort!). You never

quite know what's in store. A track may start as good, hard-packed gravel, but then degrade to a rougher, rockier affair, or, most hard-going of all, a muddy, hoof-churned quagmire. Despite their perils, unsurfaced byways are a surefire way of getting away from it all, if that's your desire.

The roads, tracks and byways of Central England offer almost unlimited possibilities for wayfaring by bicycle. The purpose of this book is not to offer a comprehensive inventory of lost lanes but to showcase some of the best, and to take you to some beautiful and interesting new places. I hope you will adapt and refine my routes according to your own tastes, and devise entirely new routes of your own. Once you get your eye in, you'll soon be amassing your own compendium of lost lanes. Good exploring!

Jack Thurston, February 2022

Lincolnshire Wolds

MAPS AND NAVIGATION

MAPS AND ELEVATION PROFILES

The maps in the book are at a scale of just over 1:152,000. Therefore 1 cm on the map is about 1.5 km on the road and 1 inch on the map is about 2.3 miles. On the elevation profiles, 1 cm is about 400 metres of climbing and 1 inch is about 3,300 feet.

ONLINE DIRECTIONS & GPX FILES

This is a heavy book, and the last thing anyone would want to do is carry it around for a day's cycling. That's why all the information needed to ride the routes is available on the Lost Lanes website. The table on page 10 provides a website address for each ride where these resources can be found. Here you will find Ordnance Survey maps and printable route sheets with turn-by-turn directions. There are also GPX files for use with GPS navigation devices and instructions for how to use these with smartphone navigation apps.

HEARTLANDS

———

In sketching this portrait of Central England I have deliberately chosen a large canvas. As well as including the traditional core of the Midlands, it covers an area from the Cotswolds to the Peak District, and from Lincolnshire to the Welsh border. I am aware that this takes in a few places that some consider to be Northern, and an entire county that the Government views as part of the South-West. As justification for drawing the lines where I have, I invoke no less powerful an authority than the once-mighty Kingdom of Mercia. For three centuries Mercia was the richest and most successful of the seven Anglo-Saxon kingdoms that emerged between the fall of the Roman Empire and the Norman Conquest. Though more than a thousand years ago, their names still echo in the mental geography of this island: Northumbria, East Anglia, Wessex, Essex, Kent and Sussex. Scotland to the north, Wales to the west, and right there in the middle, Mercia.

Paradoxically, the name Mercia is derived from the Old English *Merce*, and means 'people of the borders'. The borders in question were with the Celtic Britons the Mercians had driven to the west (beyond King Offa's famous dyke), and with the Kingdom of Northumbria (i.e. 'north of the Humber'). The River Thames formed Mercia's southern border with Wessex. Following the shock of the Viking invasion, a long fightback led by King Alfred of Wessex saw Mercia regain its lost lands and the unification of all the Anglo-Saxons into a new kingdom of England. The land of the Mercians has been in the thick of the action ever since, witnessing the dynastic struggles of the Wars of the Roses, the religious upheavals of the Reformation and the decisive battles of the Civil War. But the region's greatest era — a time of truly global significance — was when it became the fiery crucible of Britain's industrial revolution.

AN EXPLOSION OF INGENUITY

Accidents of nature provided the raw materials for its earliest industries, from the salt springs of Droitwich to the veins of lead in hills of the Peak District, the iron, coal and lime in the rock strata at Coalbrookdale, the fast-flowing streams that powered the earliest cotton mills and the mineral-rich waters of Burton-on-Trent that are perfect for brewing pale ale. But natural resources would have been nothing without a less tangible ingredient, the spark of invention. The cascade of innovative new ideas in science, engineering, economics and political thought produced by the people of the Midlands of the 1700s is down to the unusually close and creative relationships between the region's leading scientists, philosophers and entrepreneurs.

The key nexus of the so-called Midlands Enlightenment was the Lunar Society, a Birmingham dinner club and informal learned society that met during the full moon, when the extra light made the journey home easier and safer. Among its most colourful members was Erasmus Darwin, who sometimes hosted meetings of the society at his house in nearby Lichfield. A philosopher, a poet and a medical doctor, Darwin was also a natural scientist and an inventor. He was the first person to give a full description of how clouds form and of photosynthesis in plants, and drew up designs for a speaking machine, a copying machine and a 'flying chariot' or aeroplane. But Lichfield's answer to Leonardo da Vinci ran into hot water with his early theory of human evolution that flatly contradicted the teachings of the Bible. Branded a crank by the establishment, it fell to his grandson Charles (born and raised not far away in Shrewsbury) to prove that Erasmus had been onto something after all.

Among the other 'Lunarticks', as the group

Ironbridge

cheerfully referred to themselves, were James Watt and Matthew Boulton in Birmingham. They not only perfected the steam engine but also pioneered the concept of mass-producing goods in a large, specialised 'manufactory'. Along with Josiah Wedgwood's world-beating pottery works in Staffordshire, and Richard Arkwright's cotton mills in the Derwent Valley, Central England led the world into the modern era of mass production and the consumer society.

It wasn't all about successful entrepreneurs and wealthy amateur scientists with laboratories in their country estates and elegant townhouses. The explosion of ingenuity was underpinned by inventive people of more modest means. Britain was an island of tinkerers and fettlers, nowhere more than in the Midlands. Its skilled craftspeople were creative, hard-working, self-reliant and independent-minded. Many were religious nonconformists such as Quakers whose founder, George Fox, came from Leicestershire. Their dissenting religion meant they were barred from elite universities and from

jobs in the government and the military. Free from the restrictive hierarchies of feudalism, courtly life, and the church, the prevailing culture was one of free-thinking and social mobility. They trusted one another and were willing to pool resources and share ideas. Abraham Darby's pioneering ironworks in Coalbrookdale owed much to the region's Quaker network. Birmingham Quaker John Cadbury founded a chocolate empire that sought to forge a more humane form of capitalism. The Bournville district of Birmingham was conceived by the Cadbury family as 'a factory in a garden' where employees were provided with good quality homes, amenities for leisure and learning and plenty of green space. It was a radical new idea that helped inspire the garden city movement. The Cadbury family also campaigned against child labour, poverty, animal cruelty and alcoholism, and founded new schools, colleges and hospitals. In the 1920s and 1930s they supported Quaker aid for European war refugees, and played a major role in setting up the Youth Hostel Association.

While John Cadbury was expanding his chocolate business, over in Leicestershire, a itinerant Baptist preacher, pamphleteer and furniture-maker named Thomas Cook had a simple idea that led to another new and successful business empire. In 1841 Cook chartered a passenger train on the recently opened railway line to take some 500 fellow temperance campaigners on a day trip from Leicester to attend a teetotal rally in nearby Loughborough. For a shilling, Cook's passengers got round trip train travel, band entertainment and refreshments. The excursion was a success and Cook never looked back, organising trips further afield. In 1851 his company took more than 150,000 people on trips to see the Great Exhibition in London and started arranging tours around Europe. As the world's first travel agency, Thomas Cook & Son expanded people's horizons and gave the middle classes a new taste for travel as leisure.

THE WHEELS OF CHANGE

At around the same time, the very first pedal-powered velocipedes were emerging from the workshop of a Parisian coach-maker. Made from wood and iron, they were incredibly heavy; the punishing ride led them to become known as 'boneshakers'. In 1868 James Starley's sewing machine company in Coventry received an order from France to manufacture 400 of these new contraptions. The outbreak of the Franco-Prussian war meant that the bikes were never delivered, but Starley had no trouble selling them on the domestic market. Sensing a business opportunity, he set about improving on the primitive French design.

New technologies like ball-bearings and wire-tension spokes led to the penny-farthings and tricycles of the first great bicycle boom in 1870s. These new machines demonstrated the true potential of human-powered locomotion, but high-wheelers were rather difficult and dangerous to ride, while tricycles were slow and cumbersome. In the 1880s Starley's nephew, John Kemp Starley, came up with a new design that was a game-changer. The Rover 'safety bicycle' possessed all the essential characteristics of the modern bicycle as we know it today: two wheels of equal size, a diamond shaped frame, steering by a handlebar connected to the forks that held the front wheel, rear-wheel drive using a chain and variable sprockets. It was safe to ride, and gave people the speed and the comfort to travel considerable distances with a genuine sense of freedom and independence quite different from the regimented tourism of the Thomas Cook model. Even so, bicycles were still expensive objects to make. Only the relatively wealthy had the money and the time to indulge in this new and wildly popular pastime. Having perfected its form, the ingenious minds of the Midlands set about making the bicycle affordable to all. In the early 1900s, Coventry was shifting into making cars (Rover cars inherited the name from Rover bicycles) and the leading cycle manufacturers were based in Birmingham and Nottingham, though there were bicycle and component factories spread right across the region. The likes of BSA, Hercules and Raleigh vied for the crown of the world's biggest bicycle manufacturer, and output rose year on year.

Meanwhile, another Midlands invention was opening up the countryside to these new self-propelled voyagers. In 1901, while out walking, Edgar Hooley, the chief surveyor for Nottinghamshire County Council, noticed an unusually smooth stretch of road near a Derbyshire ironworks. Locals told him that a barrel of tar had fallen from a cart onto the road, and someone had poured waste slag from the blast furnaces to cover up the mess. The result was a smooth and solid road surface with none of the ruts and dust that plagued the gravel road surfaces of the time. Hooley perfected the process of combining slag with heated tar, adding stones to the mixture to create a smooth and durable road surface. Radcliffe Road in Nottingham was the world's first tarmac road; Hooley's invention enabled cyclists of the inter-war years to explore further, in greater comfort and on ever lighter and faster machines.

Britain's love affair with the bicycle reached its peak in the early 1950s. The country was producing 3.5 million bicycles a year. More than a quarter of British people cycled to work and more than a third of people living in rural areas used bicycles as their main mode of transport. For cycle tourists,

Birmingham

Newark

River Severn

Peak District

Worcestershire

Lincolnshire Wolds

Central England was a paradise, with its gentle countryside, labyrinth of lanes, pubs and tea-rooms in every town and village and a growing network of youth hostels for overnight stays. A typical day out was captured in the short film *Cyclists' Special* in which groups of cyclists take a specially chartered train from London to Rugby for a day out riding in the heart of England. It is available to watch on YouTube and will have you yearning for the simpler times of steel bikes, leather saddles, stylish attire, no helmets and barely any cars on the roads.

It was in this golden era of cycling that a teenage girl growing up in wartime Coventry joined friends, who shared her taste for adventure, riding out of the bombed-out city centre to explore the Warwickshire countryside. After Eileen Sheridan had completed the classic '140 miles in 12 hours' cycle-touring challenge, she started entering races, and was soon winning them. Though just 4 feet 11 inches tall she set national new records in time trials from 30 miles all the way up to 12 hours. Dubbed "the mighty atom", Sheridan signed a lucrative professional contract with Hercules of Birmingham and broke every place-to-place record on the books. By the end of her 1954 Land's End to John O'Groats record ride of 2 days, 11 hours and 7 minutes she was so cold and exhausted she was hallucinating phantoms and polar bears by the roadside and had to be spoon-fed. Her record was unbroken for 36 years. I have had the honour of meeting Eileen and she remains an inspiration as a remarkable athlete and as one of the great trailblazing women in sport. Her record-breaking bike is on display in the Coventry Transport Museum.

SHIRES, MIRES, SPIRES AND SQUIRES

Topographically, Central England is a shallow bowl with higher ground on three of its four sides. To the north are the Peak District and the Staffordshire Moorlands, to the south the Cotswolds and the Northamptonshire Escarpment. To the west are hills that rise towards the Welsh border, but to the east is the North Sea coast. Into this bowl flow Britain's longest and third-longest rivers: the Severn from the hills of Mid-Wales, and the Trent from the Staffordshire moorlands. Their watersheds are separated by the slight dome on which stand Birmingham and the Black Country.

Both the Severn and the Trent have shaped the landscape through which they flow. The Severn once flowed north towards the Mersey, but during the last Ice Age it was blocked by an advancing northern glacier. The water built up into a lake that now forms the flat lands of Shropshire and the Cheshire Plain. The lake eventually overflowed southwards, creating the Ironbridge Gorge and a new course for the Severn via the Bristol Channel. The Trent once flowed due east across Lincolnshire into the North Sea but it was also blocked by a mass of ice that lay on what is now the Vale of Belvoir. The water was forced into another giant lake which emptied into the Humber Estuary.

Many of the region's most important medieval cities and towns grew up at strategic crossing points along these two rivers and their tributaries. Shrewsbury, Worcester, Tewkesbury and Gloucester are all on the banks of the Severn, while Stoke, Burton, Nottingham and Newark are on the Trent. Even today there are several long stretches of river without a crossing point, which creates challenges for route-planning. Both rivers remain shapeshifters, meandering extravagantly across their flood plains and regularly bursting their banks after heavy rain. Central England's network of rivers and man-made canals turbocharged the early phase of the industrial revolution until they were largely superseded by steam-powered railways.

The legacy of these transport networks today is more miles of rideable canal towpaths and rails-to-trails routes than in any other part of Britain. The most spectacular of these are in the southern half of the Peak District. Its canals and disused railways overlay a dense network of old roads, green lanes and packhorse trails. No area of Britain combines such a high density of routes for exploring by bike with such stunning landscapes, from windswept moors of purple heather and vertiginous gritstone edges to limestone crags and caverns. On its dales and upland plateaus, a vast patchwork of small fields includes a staggering 5,440 miles of dry-stone walls. Within easy reach of so many industrial towns and cities, it's no wonder that the Peak District was the focal point for campaigns for greater land access and the right to roam. Those battles, including dramatic physical confrontations between ramblers and gamekeepers, led to the creation of Britain's first national park. Today, some 20 million people live within an hour's journey of the Peak District. Its tourist honeypots sometimes heave with visitors, but with a bicycle it's still easy to find peace and solitude within a few minutes' ride.

The Shropshire Hills are the region's other big expanse of upland and open country. Some of the oldest and most unusual geology in England makes the area a mecca for rock hounds and cyclists with a taste for climbing. Shropshire has five peaks over 500m high. The county tops of Herefordshire and Worcestershire are both over 400m. Elsewhere, isolated local prominences like Cleeve Hill and May Hill in Gloucestershire, Ebrington Hill and the Burton Dassett Hills in Warwickshire, Bredon Hill in Worcestershire and the Wrekin in Shropshire all have views much bigger than their altitudes would lead you to think. And most have a road or a rideable track that will take you to the very top.

But there's no hiding the fact that Lincolnshire and Nottinghamshire are among the flattest counties in England. As if to rub it in, the highest point is the man-made spoil heap of the former Silverhill colliery which rises to 205m. Much of Lincolnshire is barely above sea level, though the crest of the Wolds *feels* higher and hillier than its greatest elevation of 168m. The Lincolnshire coast is one vast expanse of dune-backed mud flats and wind farms. There is a string of broad sandy beaches, including traditional bucket-and-spade resorts like Skegness and Cleethorpes, protected

Though largely arable today, the core of the Cotswolds was once home to vast flocks of sheep. Wool was the oil that fuelled the economy of medieval England. The wealth generated is still on show in the fine houses of wool merchants and the extravagant architecture of the richly-endowed 'wool churches'. North-east of the Cotswolds, the hills are gentler and the soils more fertile. The combination of high-quality agricultural land, abundant building stone, good transport connections and plenty of open space to hunt wild animals are the reasons why this swathe of Northamptonshire, Leicestershire and Nottinghamshire have so many large landed estates. The immense wealth derived from large landholdings, sometimes enriched by the spoils of colonialism and slavery, is expressed in grand country houses set in elegant landscaped parkland.

Dotted across Central England are some of the landscapes that have inspired some of England's greatest literature. Although Shakespeare wrote primarily for a London audience, he divided his time between the city and his home town of Stratford-upon-Avon. His plays are dotted with places, people and events from the Warwickshire countryside. His duality as a man equally at home in the fields and villages of rural England and the metropolis of Elizabethan London adds richness and depth to Shakespeare's genius as poet, dramatist and observer of the human condition.

D. H. Lawrence, the first great English novelist with truly working class roots, was a cyclist himself, if largely by economic necessity, though a short passage in Sons and Lovers captures the reckless thrill of riding at speed and, characteristically, his thoughts on its sexual significance. For Lawrence, the rural hinterland of the Nottinghamshire coalfield was "the country of my heart". He delighted in the details of Eastwood and its environs and felt its deeper resonances, once writing that "the mines were, in a sense, an accident in the landscape, and Robin Hood and his merry men were not very far away". George Eliot was born and raised in Nuneaton and she set *Middlemarch*, her greatest novel (for some, the greatest of all English novels), in a fictitious Midlands town. In *The Mill on the Floss*,

nature reserves and off-limits military firing ranges. Inland, Central England's largest county is a bracing, big-sky landscape of marsh, fen and wold. As a landscape it could not be further removed from the intricate labyrinth of hills, lush valleys, small fields and wooded dells in Shropshire, Herefordshire and the areas of Worcestershire and Gloucestershire west of the River Severn.

East of the Severn, in Gloucestershire and southern Warwickshire is the geological feature that marks the boundary between Central and Southern England. It gives rise to one of the most celebrated English landscapes. The Cotswolds are a part of the broad and intermittent outcrop of limestone that extends from Lyme Bay in Dorset to the Cleveland Hills in North Yorkshire. The escarpment rises almost imperceptibly from the south-east to form a broad plateau with steep-sided valleys and a dramatic crest overlooking the Severn and the Vale of Evesham. The honey-toned limestone dates from the Jurassic period, when dinosaurs ruled the Earth and the first birds were just taking to the skies. It is the fossilised remains of a shallow tropical sea that once teemed with aquatic life.

Kerne Bridge

the River Trent brings the story to its tragic climax. *Lord of the Rings* author J. R. R. Tolkien — who grew up in and around Birmingham and its suburbs — described The Shire, the idyllic homeland of the Hobbits, as "more or less a Warwickshire village" of the 1890s.

In certain respects, England's overbearing North-South divide has left Central England as the squeezed middle. Midlanders' typical reticence when it comes to blowing their own trumpets is an admirable trait, but it hasn't exactly helped the region hold its ground against the economic and political might of the South-East and the powerful regional identity of the North. The cultures of the Midlands are so diverse that they elude simple categorisation. As Alan Sillitoe's fictional creation, Arthur Seaton, who worked tedious shifts in the Raleigh bicycle factory in Nottingham, famously declared, "I'm me and nobody else; and whatever people think I am or say I am, that's what I'm not, because they don't know a bloody thing about me." The hedonistic anti-hero of *Saturday Night and Sunday Morning* is part of Nottinghamshire's rebel tradition, from Robin Hood to the strike-defying

coal miners of the 1980s and the stark beats and abrasive rants of Sleaford Mods. By most accounts, Birmingham and the Black Country is the birthplace of heavy metal, producing Black Sabbath, Judas Priest and half the members of Led Zeppelin. Worlds apart musically, but no less rebellious and just as deeply rooted in the West Midlands, was Coventry's multi-racial, 2-Tone scene that included The Specials, The Selecter and The Beat, and Birmingham pop-reggae superstars UB40.

The Chinese word for China, Zhōngguó (中國), literally means 'the country — or kingdom — in the middle'. Similarly, most of the great civilisations in and around the Mediterranean thought of this as the 'middle sea'. There is pride and prestige in being at the heart of things. From the deep gorges of the Wye Valley to the heights of Lincolnshire Wolds, from small but perfectly formed Rutland to the magnificent wildness of the Shropshire hills, from the charm of the Cotswolds to the crags and cliffs of the Peak District, and everywhere that lies in between, Central England is a vast and varied territory to explore. You can't miss it. It's bang in the middle.

BEFORE YOU GO

PRACTICALITIES

———

ROUTES AND MAPS

The rides in this book range from 25 to 65 miles but most are around the 35- to 50-mile mark, which for most people is a good distance for a leisurely day's ride, or a half-day ride for the energetic. I've deliberately refrained from adding any timing to the rides, as it's better to ride at one's own pace than somebody else's. However, based on a typical touring pace of 10 to 12 miles per hour, allowing for hills, most rides require 4 to 6 hours in the saddle. If, like me, your idea of a good day out on the bike includes taking time to stop for a pub lunch or a cream tea (or both!), a river dip and an afternoon nap, then ending the day by scrambling up a hill to watch the sunset, you may want to split the longer rides over a couple of days. To this end, I've recommended good places to spend the night, along with the listings of recommended pubs, cafés and bike shops. A night in a grand coaching inn or a boutique B&B is lovely, but some of my best bike overnights were spent out in the open, tucked up in a bivvy bag looking up at the stars.

Despite its reputation as fairly flat country, there are plenty of hills in Central England, and especially in its most scenic corners. Hills have a significant impact on the time and effort required to ride a given distance. A decent basic level of fitness is required for some of the hillier rides. I've indicated the total vertical ascent of each ride, which should give a clue as to how hilly it is; the elevation profiles will also help. The secret is to pace yourself, and not be in too much of a hurry. If a hill feels too much to ride, there's absolutely no shame in walking.

The maps in the book are best used in combination with a good paper map, such as the Ordnance Survey's peerless 1:50,000 Landranger series. The cost of buying them does add up, but they can be borrowed from most public libraries or viewed and printed online from Bing.com/maps. The Ordnance Survey's own smartphone app and third-party apps like BackCountry Navigator are viable alternatives to carrying paper Landranger maps. When planning rides, I look as far as possible for the narrowest class of unclassified lane, those that are less than 4m in width. This is so narrow that two cars cannot pass without slowing to a near stop, or waiting in a passing place. On Landranger maps they are indicated as the narrower of the two types of road coloured in yellow.

As well as the maps in the book, there is a printable route sheet and a GPS navigation file for each ride on the Lost Lanes website (*lostlanes.co.uk*). Each ride has its own web page and these are listed in the table on page 10.

GPS NAVIGATION

GPS navigation is less good for exploring and improvising than a paper map, but it excels when following a pre-planned route, assuming the batteries don't run out. Cycling-oriented GPS units will alert you if you make a wrong turn and, as well as a little map, the more modern models will give you an elevation profile so you know where the hills are coming up. For each ride in the book (except the organised group rides) the web page above includes a GPX file for use in a GPS device or smartphone. For plotting new routes online, I recommend *ridewithgps.com* and *cycle.travel* as they include a good selection of maps and satellite imagery, have intuitive user interfaces and clever routing algorithms. Garmin has long been the market leader in cycling GPS devices but I've had very good experience with a Wahoo ELEMNT device while researching this book. Smartphones also provide GPS navigation and the

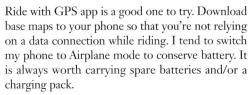

Ride with GPS app is a good one to try. Download base maps to your phone so that you're not relying on a data connection while riding. I tend to switch my phone to Airplane mode to conserve battery. It is always worth carrying spare batteries and/or a charging pack.

TAKE THE TRAIN

I have tried to make the rides accessible by train. Two Together and Family and Friends railcards offer big savings. Breaking a return journey is a good way to get more value from a single fare, and most rail companies allow unlimited breaking on the return leg of an open return journey, including overnight breaks, so long as the ticket is still valid (they are usually valid for one month). For a few days away, a Rover ticket may be a good option. Trains tend to have between two and six dedicated bicycle spaces, and booking in advance is the best way to secure a stress-free journey and avoid disappointment. Most inter-city services now require cycle reservations, though these can sometimes be done up to 15 minutes before travelling or via a smartphone app. Some train companies restrict access to trains during peak commuting times when they are at their busiest. If the train already has its full complement of bikes or, if you've not made a reservation, a pleading look and heartfelt gratitude can work wonders. Most train conductors are human.

ANY KIND OF BIKE

The rides in this book can be ridden on any bike that's in good mechanical order and the right size for the rider. Low gears make climbing hills much less like hard work. A triple chainring, a sub-compact double and/or a 34-tooth or greater rear sprocket can tame the steepest gradient. Tyre choice makes a huge difference to comfort. Good-quality tyres between 28mm and 47mm wide are a sensible all-round choice for a fast and comfortable ride. Avoid really knobbly tyres as they slow you down on tarmac roads. A steel touring bike is an ideal choice. There is plenty of choice from brands including Ridgeback, Genesis, Trek and Spa Cycles. The new style of gravel and adventure bikes are perfect if you're travelling light. These bikes have the look and feel of a road bike but with disc brakes that perform well in all weathers, nice wide tyres and all the fittings for luggage and mudguards.

Unless it's the middle of a heatwave, I consider mudguards an essential item: it's bad enough being rained on from above; it's worse to have a jet of mucky water sprayed up from below. Check the weather forecast and prepare accordingly (smartphone weather apps are very handy). It's no fun pushing on through a monsoon; better to take cover until the storm passes, as they usually do.

LIGHTS, LOCKS & LUGGAGE

When riding in the dark, a set of lights is a legal requirement. Even if you don't plan to ride in the dark, packing a set of lights is a useful precaution just in case your ride takes longer than planned. Modern battery-powered LED lights are nothing short of amazing. A power bank is also handy if your phone, lights or GPS device needs topping up. Dynamo lighting is making a revival, and there are special adaptors to use the power from a hub dynamo to recharge a power bank. If you plan to ride at night, then some reflective material is also helpful, in addition to lights. In the countryside, a lock is often unnecessary but is a sensible precaution, especially if you plan to leave your bicycle unattended for any length of time. A small cable 'café lock' is enough to deter an opportunist, but in cities or large towns where professional bike thieves may be lurking, it makes sense to pack a heavier, more secure lock. If riding with others, a single lock can secure several bikes.

Money, a basic tool kit, a snack and a mobile phone can be stuffed into a very small rucksack, bumbag or in the rear pockets of a cycling jersey. Anything heavier is more comfortable if carried on the bicycle itself, in either a handlebar bag, a saddlebag or a pannier. When out for an all-day ride it's wise to carry a frame-mounted water bottle or two. Refill as you go: pubs and cafés are happy to oblige their customers and many churches and village halls have an outside tap.

CLOTHING AND SHOES

In spite of the images of Lycra-clad professional bike racers (and their amateur lookalikes) in magazines and on television, the overwhelming majority of people in the world who ride bikes do so in ordinary clothing. Of course, there's nothing wrong with indulging in the latest cycling fashions or donning a cycling uniform of one kind or another, but the reality is that whatever clothing is comfortable for a walk in the park will be fine for riding a bike in the countryside for a few hours. Padded shorts or underwear provide extra comfort if needed. Tight jeans with raised seams can be uncomfortable on longer rides. In heavy rain, thick cotton and denim gets waterlogged, won't keep you warm, and takes longer to dry than woollens and synthetic fibres. Riding in the rain isn't much fun but lightweight, waterproof fabrics are a big improvement over old-style plastic pac-a-macs. For night rides and camping trips, a few extra layers are a good idea, as well as a warm hat. From autumn to spring, windproof gloves keep fingers nice and warm. I am a fan of the outdoor clothing companies Páramo and Patagonia. Both make outstanding, long-lasting gear and put ethical manufacturing and environmental responsibility at the heart of their businesses.

Cycling-specific shoes are unnecessary for all but the most speed-oriented cyclists. The way I see it, large, flat pedals with good grip mean I can wear almost any type of shoe. But if you like the feeling of 'clipping in' I'm not going to argue.

WHEN THINGS GO WRONG

Compared to running a car, the cost of maintaining a bicycle, even if all the work is done by a professional bike mechanic, is minuscule. Assuming the bicycle is in generally good mechanical order, the skills and tools necessary to mend a puncture and fix a dropped chain are enough to guarantee self-sufficiency on day rides. A truly worst-case scenario means phoning for a taxi to the nearest train station.

A basic on-the-road repair kit consists of the following:
• Tyre levers, a pump and a couple of spare inner tubes
• A puncture repair kit
• Screwdrivers and hex keys required for removing wheels, adjusting brakes and tightening racks, mudguard fittings and the seat-post clamp
• A few cable ties (zip ties) can come in handy in emergencies, and a bungee cord is useful for securing bikes on trains.

Learning a little about how a bike works not only saves money but comes with a warm, satisfying glow of self-sufficiency. Some tasks are best left to a professional, but the basics are easily mastered. If there's nobody around to give a hands-on lesson, buy a bike maintenance book or look online for instructional videos, such as those by Patrick Field at *youtube.com/madegoodfilms*.

RIDING SAFE AND SOUND

Riding a safe distance (at least 0.5m/1.5ft) from the roadside and at least a car door's width from any parked cars is much safer than hugging the kerb. Making eye contact with other road users helps everyone get along.

On roads, it is cyclists who suffer most from the boorish attitude that 'might makes right', but we should be at pains to preserve the civility of traffic-free paths shared with walkers, skaters and horse riders. Be aware that other people are out enjoying themselves, too, and may not be paying full attention. Approach horse riders with caution and a friendly verbal greeting to let the beast know that you're human.

When leading group rides with slower or less experienced cyclists, rather than speed off and leave the group trailing in your wake, aim to ride at a pace that's no faster than the slowest riders can comfortably manage, and make plenty of stops for short breaks.

CLUBS AND ORGANISATIONS

Membership of Cycling UK (CUK), British Cycling or your local cycling campaign group not only helps these worthy organisations campaign on behalf of cyclists but also brings benefits like discounts in bike shops, member magazines, third-party insurance and free legal advice in the very unlikely event of an accident. Most local cycling groups have programmes of free or very nearly free social rides, which are a great way of discovering new places and meeting new people. An experienced ride leader will take care of all the navigation, and planning tea and lunch stops.

There are also good online communities of cyclists. The CUK web forum brims with expert touring and technical advice and Bear Bones Bikepacking is a good place to find out more about bikepacking in the UK. They are both lively communities to ask for advice, to find out about rides, routes and events, and even to find riding companions. Warm Showers is a free hospitality exchange for touring cyclists. Founded in 1955, the Rough Stuff Fellowship continues to celebrate cycling on unsurfaced paths, tracks and byways.

The National Trust and English Heritage maintain hundreds of amazing properties across the country, but entry fees can be high if you're just making a fleeting visit while out for a day's bike ride. If you're the kind of person who enjoys visiting historic buildings and sumptuous gardens, an annual membership makes sense and all funds help contribute to the upkeep of their properties. Similarly, the RSPB, the Wildlife Trusts and Plantlife are member-funded charities that do important work conserving and restoring the natural environment and maintain some superb nature reserves.

Finally, another way to immerse yourself in all things bicycle is to listen to The Bike Show, the long-running cycling podcast that I present (*thebikeshow.net*).

BEST FOR

WILD CAMPING

There's no greater contentment than sitting out under the stars, well-fed, feeling a gentle night breeze on your face, with no other disturbance than an owl hooting in the nearby woods or sheep bleating in the valley below. Whether alone and enjoying a moment of peace and solitude or having a good time with friends, the cares of day-to-day life are left far behind. Many of the routes in this book could be used as the basis for a short overnight trip with a bivvy bag or lightweight tent.

Though wild camping is legal in Scotland, this is not the case in England and Wales, with the exception of parts of Dartmoor, where it is legal, and the fells of the Lake District, where it is accepted as a long-standing tradition. In theory, one should ask for permission from the landowner but it is difficult to know who owns any given piece of land, and not always easy to find them. I take the pragmatic view that if I'm out of sight of roads, farms and houses, and careful to leave absolutely no trace other than a patch of flattened grass, no landowner will mind, or even know, that I've spent the night.

But there's a more radical perspective. The idea that land ownership is absolute, and includes the right to physically exclude other people, is surprisingly recent. It dates from the 'age of enclosure' that got going in the mid-1700s. At the time it was intensely controversial. As the son of a Midland farm labourer, the poet John Clare was an eye-witness to enclosure and decried its injustices, mourning the loss in time when "Unbounded freedom ruled the wandering scene / Nor fence of ownership crept in between". The philosopher John Stuart Mill argued that "No man made the land, it is the original inheritance of the whole species. The land of every country belongs to the people of that country." Wild camping hardly compares to the many violent protests against land enclosure in the 18th and 19th centuries, nor to the occupation of land by the likes of the Levellers and the Diggers, nor even the famous mass trespasses on Winter Hill in 1896 and Kinder Scout in 1932. Yet it remains a peaceful act of resistance and a powerful reconnection with lost liberties.

DO IT YOURSELF

Central England lacks the large, sparsely populated expanses where it's so easy to find good wild camping spots. But it is still entirely possible: in areas of upland like the Peak District and the Shropshire Hills; in woods and open heath; and on uncultivated field margins. Often the best spots are accessible from bridleways, byways or footpaths rather than the road. A little prep work can help. Look at the Ordnance Survey's 1:25,000 (Explorer) maps together with satellite imagery to get an idea of the terrain (they're both available free online at *bing.com/maps*). Google Street View is handy for checking out the lie of the land, and *geograph.org.uk* is a useful source of images. When out on day rides, I often make a mental note of a potential camping spot for a future overnight trip. When choosing a spot be sure not to disturb livestock or trample crops or ecologically sensitive habitats such as bluebell woods, and definitely don't light a campfire.

The bivvy bag is the ultimate tool for stealth camping and the sense of sleeping beneath the stars, but it's not to everyone's taste. A tent gives a sense of security and more protection from the elements and from midges, but adds weight and can make you more conspicuous. Sleeping under a tarp is a popular halfway house between tent

and bivvy bag. Some people swear by hammocks. It's all a matter of taste. If you've not wild camped before, the easiest way to give it a try is to go for a single night, ideally in clear, calm and warm weather. If you forget something, it's no big deal as you'll be returning to 'civilisation' the next day. To avoid detection, choose a site well away from the road or any places where people live, arrive fairly late in the day and get going early the next morning.

Rather than bother to cook an elaborate camp dinner, for summertime one-nighters I tend to fill a Thermos flask with something hot from home — a stew, fried rice, curry or a hearty soup. I might take a lightweight camping stove to boil water for couscous or dried noodles and a hot drink in the morning. Having enough water with you is important and requires a little planning. Two large bike bottles per person allows plenty for drinking while riding, some for cooking in the evening and enough for tea or coffee in the morning. If you do run dry, most pubs will be happy to refill your bottles, many village halls and churches have an outside tap, or you could just knock at a door. If taking water from rivers or streams, a portable water filter or purification tablets are a sensible precaution. Leave no trace. Even better, leave the land in a better state than you found it by collecting any litter left by others.

No. 7 NATURAL HIGH

The western lobe of the Peak District is less heavily visited than the east, and so finding a hideaway to wild camp is that much easier. The Goyt Valley is one option, with good paths around the ruins of Errwood Hall. The rocky outcrops around the Roaches have wonderful sunset views, though finding a flat piece of ground out of the wind isn't always easy.

No. 9 SHROPSHIRE THRILLS

The wide open spaces of the Long Mynd and the Stiperstones have plenty of spots that are suitable for a bivvy or a wild camp, though it is wise to choose a calm day. They're both high and exposed locations, and the weather can get wild.

No. 14 ROADS LESS TRAVELLED BY

The long ridge of Marcle Hill and Ridge Hill has sections of bridleway and footpath which are perfect bivvy spots, with good views at both sunset and sunrise. At the southern end of the route is May Hill, a broad hill crowned by a grove of Scots pines, from where the views are exceptional. The hill is owned by the National Trust and, as a popular beauty spot, a measure of discretion is required. On May morning you'll be woken by Morris dancers and neo-pagans who gather here to greet the sunrise.

No. 15 FREEDOM OF THE FOREST

The Forest of Dean is so large that it's no trouble to slip away into the woods for a night of wild camping. The Forest is home to the Britain's largest population of wild boar. These large and powerful animals keep themselves to themselves, but you might hear one in the night — it's an ungodly sound, part growl, part roar, part snort. This route also includes tracks beside the River Wye and the promise of a bracing morning swim to start the day.

No. 21 CUT TO THE CHASE

Cannock Chase might be one of the most popular open spaces in the West Midlands, but it is easily big enough to find an out-of-the-way spot for a wild camp. It's owned by Staffordshire County Council so the chances of encountering an irate gamekeeper are minimal. Though, as a supposed hotspot of paranormal activity, you may have other things to look out for, from phantoms and ghoulish apparitions to UFOs.

NO. 25 HIGHER GROUND

The density of gated roads, byways and bridleways in this part of Leicestershire means it's quite easy to steal away onto a field margin with a small tent, tarp or bivvy bag. It helps to identify a likely spot well ahead of time, so you're not hunting in the dark. Head to a country pub for a pint, a bite and a refill of bottles and then, in the words of Ivor Cutler, just go to a field to lie down.

No. 28 THE WAY THROUGH THE WOODS

Much of this route is on forest trails so there are plenty of possibilities to find a secluded spot to unfurl a bivvy bag or sling a hammock between trees and make like Robin Hood or Maid Marian. To avoid detection or disturbance, be sure to keep well away from the trail, and be mindful of the ecology of this ancient woodland.

BEST FOR

WILD SWIMMING

It is scientifically proven that you can revive tired leg muscles by submerging them in cold water. I've used this trick any number of times when tired towards the end of a ride and it really works. Whether a brief bracing dip in an upland stream or waterfall or a more relaxing float among lily-pads or a gentle drift down a slowly meandering river, wild swimming clears the mind and leaves your body tingling all over. Regular cold water immersion improves blood circulation, reduces inflammation of muscles, boosts the immune system and can even help with weight loss by increasing the body's metabolic rate.

Before swimming pools, of course, all swimming was wild swimming. But like so many aspects of our relationship with the natural world, it fell into a long decline. The nature writer Roger Deakin's 1999 book *Waterlog: A Swimmer's Journey Through Britain* sparked a revival of interest and there is now a large and growing community of open water swimmers. Once you've enjoyed a swim in a lake or a river, an indoor swimming pool, with its chlorinated water and strip lighting, will feel like a very pale imitation of the real thing.

From the gin-clear limestone streams of the Peak District to the mighty Severn and Wye and smaller rivers like the Avon and the Nene there are lots of places on rides in this book that are perfect for a plunge. Basic precautions to stay safe include being alert to the strength of the river's flow and the depth of the water. Very cold water can be a dangerous shock to the unprepared so check the temperature before jumping straight in, or go in gradually.

Sadly, some big rivers like the Severn, the Trent and the Wye are suffering from pollution from agricultural run-off upstream and, occasionally, the dumping of untreated sewage by miscreant water companies. Trust your own judgment. If the water looks appealing, it is probably clean enough to swim. If it looks unappealing (gloopy, scummy or cloudy), or it smells wrong, trust your instinct to stay out. To clean things up, lend your voice to campaigns for stronger regulation against water pollution. Daniel Start's *Wild Swimming* and *Wild Swimming Coast* are comprehensive guides, listing over 700 of the best swimming locations.

River Lathkill at Conksbury bridge

River Dove at Mappleton bridge

No. 1 PEAK PLEASURE

The limestone country of the White Peak has some fantastic spots for a paddle or a refreshing plunge, if not a full-scale swim, and this route passes several. The first is in the River Bradford, just down the hill from Youlgreave, which is popular and very safe. There is another over the hill in the River Lathkill. The River Wye is good for paddling at Ashford-in-the-Water and total immersion is eminently possible either upstream or downstream of the Monsal Head viaduct, from where there are paths down to the water's edge.

No. 5 MANIFOLD DESTINY

There are popular swim spots in the River Dove near the beginning of this ride (by the bridge between Norbury and Ellastone) and towards the end, under Okeover Bridge near Mapleton. Both are accessible by riverside footpaths. Another lovely, and popular, spot for a paddle and a dip is at the Stepping Stones in Dove Dale. This is a scenic 1½ mile detour from Ilam to the Dove Dale car park and on up the tarmac track (cycling is permitted).

No. 11 TAKE IT TO THE BRIDGE

The Severn is a big river and should be treated with respect. If you're an experienced open water swimmer and the river isn't in flood, it's eminently possible. This ride passes swim spots at Cressage Bridge (access by footpath from the road), at Ironbridge, beneath the famous bridge itself (there are entry and exit points at Dale End and Severnside) and at innumerable spots from the riverbank upstream of Bridgnorth. Astley Abbotts is just one option.

No. 15 FREEDOM OF THE FOREST

Just like the Severn, the Wye should only be swum by confident open water swimmers and at times when the water is flowing calmly. In fine weather people swim at Symonds Yat, near the rope bridge at The Biblins, and around Redbrook, with some especially good spots accessible from the forest track on the west bank of the river. Exercise caution and look out for fishermen. A calmer and more child-friendly option is a paddle in Cannop Ponds in the Forest of Dean.

River Nene at Fotheringhay

River Wye at Monmouth

No. 19 ESCAPE VELOCITY

The Avon is a lovely swimming river and there is a good spot just off the route at Hampton Lucy. From Charlecote Mill (a working water mill) there is a bridleway across the fields. Cross the stream to reach the secluded beaches and swim spots beyond the weir.

No. 24 SMALL IS BEAUTIFUL

Swimming in Rutland Water is restricted to designated locations such as the beach at Sykes Lane near Empingham, but the River Nene provides a very pleasant alternative. There are spots at Fotheringhay just beneath the remains of the castle, and by the bridge at Oundle. The rowing club has pontoons for easy entry and exit from the water.

BEST FOR

FAMILIES

———

Traffic-free cycling is the best way for children and novice cyclists to build confidence on the bike. Sharing even quiet country lanes with motor traffic can be unnerving, especially for parents riding with young children. Fortunately, Central England has some excellent traffic-free cycle trails, thanks to the campaigning work of Sustrans and the efforts of enlightened local authorities, the Canals and Rivers Trust, the Forestry Commission and some large landowners like the National Trust. The Midlands was the heart of Georgian England's canal network and many towpaths have been upgraded as cycling and walking routes. Disused branch railways and old mineral tramways now enjoy a second life as traffic-free cycling and walking paths, especially in areas with an industrial history, such as the Peak District, the Forest of Dean, and the former coal mining areas of Nottinghamshire, Derbyshire, Staffordshire and Leicestershire.

Though the rides in this book are not suitable for young children or absolute beginners to ride in their entirety, several have sections that are perfect as stand-alone routes for younger and less experienced cyclists, and for people whose mileage is limited. These tend to be linear out-and-back routes but there are a few circular rides too.

No. 4 HAPPY TRAILS
The 17-mile High Peak Trail and the 13-mile Tissington Trail are among the best rails-to-trails projects in Britain, and are justly popular. This route takes in sections of both, as well as part of the 8-mile traffic-free path around Carsington Water. Any of these would make for a good day out for younger children, while keen teenagers might challenge themselves by taking on the entire route.

No. 5 MANIFOLD DESTINY

Opened in the 1930s, the 8-mile Manifold Way was a visionary scheme to convert a little-used railway line into a new cycling and walking path. The trail threads along the valley floor, through limestone gorges and past cliffs and caves.

No. 15 FREEDOM OF THE FOREST

The Forest of Dean's Family Trail is a 9-mile circular route following an old railway line, an ideal distance for younger children, and there's a very scenic spur between Coleford and Parkend, which adds a few more miles. This ride also includes the Peregrine Trail, from Symonds Yat to Monmouth, an 8-mile linear route beside the River Wye.

No. 24 SMALL IS BEAUTIFUL

My route takes in just a section of the largely traffic-free lakeside route around Rutland Water, but the whole thing is a great circular ride for older children and novice cyclists. At 17 miles, or 23 if you add in the Hambleton peninsular, it's just the sort of distance that's do-able yet comes with a genuine sense of achievement.

No. 28 THE WAY THROUGH THE WOODS

The well-surfaced and traffic-free trails through Clumber Park in Nottinghamshire are a joy. There are more than 20 miles of cycle routes, with the 5-mile lakeside loop especially good for beginners. The National Trust runs a cycle hub for bike hire and one-to-one lessons tailored for adults or children. A little wilder are the many forest tracks and bridleways through the greenwood of Sherwood Forest, just north-west of Edwinstowe. The coniferous plantations of Sherwood Pines are also popular, where there is a well-equipped bike hub for cycle hire, sales and servicing.

No. 29 WOLDS APART

The Water Rail Way is a 33-mile cycle route between Lincoln and Boston that is as flat as a pancake and almost completely traffic-free. The 20-mile out-and-back route from Lincoln to Bardney is a good, challenging distance for children. At Bardney, the heritage centre, with its café and fish and chip shop, is handy for a refuel at the halfway point, or could be the start point for a ride to Lincoln and back as it also has a cycle hire shop.

BEST FOR

PUBS

———

"There is nothing which has yet been contrived by man, by which so much happiness is produced as by a good tavern or inn." So wrote Samuel Johnson in 1776. As a son of Lichfield he wasn't short of a good boozer. Rural pubs have taken a beating, with a trend of closures and crude modernisations. But they seem to be fighting back, often offering good food alongside great beer. More pubs have rooms for overnight stays, or no-frills camping in a field at the back. A good country pub remains a first class destination for a bike ride.

The Midlands' association with beer runs deep. Thanks to its hard, mineral-rich spring waters and good transport connections by canal, river and rail, Burton-on-Trent once produced one in four pints drunk in Britain and exported beer around the world. Bass, Worthington's and Marston's are still going, though they are now owned by international conglomerates. The revival of small-scale brewing means there are more breweries than ever, with relative newcomers like Nottingham's Castle Rock and Thornbridge near Bakewell are now well-established alongside stalwarts like the Donnington Brewery in the Cotswolds and Bateman's in Lincolnshire. Derbyshire and the Peak District is said to have the highest concentration of micro and nano breweries in the country. Tynt Meadow, Britain's only Trappist ale, is brewed by the monks of St Bernard's Abbey in Leicestershire's Charnwood Forest.

Herefordshire, Worcestershire and Gloucestershire are a heartland of English cider and perry production. As well as big producers like Bulmers in Hereford and Westons near Ledbury, there are small-batch, seasonal cider-makers whose unpasteurised, non-carbonated 'real cider' is enjoying a quiet renaissance. And whatever you're drinking, always remember that the humble pork scratching, that quintessential pub snack, was invented and popularised in the Black Country.

No. 2 HOPE SPRINGS ETERNAL

The Barrel Inn in Bretton has one of the best views of any pub in Britain and its own heliport. Inside it's as cosy and welcoming as you could wish for, with rooms for overnight stays and a good independent hostel next door. The Anglers Rest in Bamford is a hip community-owned pub that's just off route but worth the detour.

No. 6 STAFFORDSHIRE ROLLERCOASTER

The Boat Inn at Cheddleton and the Black Lion Inn in Consall Forge are both good, friendly pubs, right by the water. Enthusiasts may want to make the detour over the hill to the Yew Tree Inn in Cauldon, an eccentric Aladdin's cave serving real ales and hearty food.

The Black Lion Inn, Consall Forge

The Royal Oak, Cardington

No. 7 NATURAL HIGH

The Staffordshire Knot in Sheen is a rustic gastropub which gets everything right, from the effortlessly stylish interior to the well-priced food. Near the end of the ride, the Hanging Gate Inn in Higher Sutton is an old drovers' inn with sunset views across the Cheshire Plain.

No. 10 OVER THE EDGE

The Royal Oak in Cardington is a 15th-century pub with bags of character: low-beamed rooms, quarry tiled floors and inglenook fireplace, and homemade pies. The Pheasant in Neenton is two miles off route, but this foodie, community-owned pub with rooms for overnight stays is well worth the detour. Post-ride pint and a bite at the stylish and spacious Ludlow Brewery.

No. 14 ROADS LESS TRAVELLED BY

The Alma Inn at Linton is a great, understated village pub serving well-kept real ales and perfectly-executed, good value pub food.

No. 15 FREEDOM OF THE FOREST

The Boat at Lower Penallt is the kind of hostelry you'd find in the Lord of the Rings. Accessible by an old railway bridge over the River Wye, it's cosy inside with a little garden that climbs up the steep, wooded valley.

The Boat Inn, Lower Penallt

No. 25 HIGHER GROUND

This ride has a pub for every taste. The Stag & Hounds in Burrough on the Hill is a friendly village pub with a Michelin Bib Gourmand. The Blue Ball in Braunston is a 17th century thatched inn while the Stilton Cheese in Somerby is a multiple CAMRA award winner.

No. 30 OUT TO LUNCH

The King's Head in Tealby claims to be the oldest thatched inn in Lincolnshire, but that would count for little if it weren't such a great pub. With a warm welcome inside, a big garden with plenty of tables, a good choice of beers and hearty food served all day, it's a justly popular landmark on the edge of the Lincolnshire Wolds.

BEST FOR

GOURMETS

There's a heartiness to the regional specialities of Central England. It's inventive, hard-working food made by and for an inventive, hard-working people. Pies loom large. Perhaps most famous of all is the pork pie, of which there are two variants: the classic, upright 'Leicestershire' with its rich, firm-yet-yielding neatly fluted pastry shell filled with cured pork; and the more rustic, hand-raised and slightly rounded 'Melton Mowbray' which is traditionally filled with uncured pork. Both are generally eaten cold but sometimes, still a little warm from the oven. Less well-known is fidget — or fidgety — pie from Shropshire and Derbyshire. This is made with a filling of pork, apples, onions and sultanas with various herbs and spices, topped by shortcrust pastry or mashed potato and served hot or cold. In a similar vein, Gloucestershire's squab pie combines leftover cuts of meat with apples, onions and root vegetables. One Midlands pie you're unlikely to encounter is the Nottinghamshire's Budby pie, which comprises cuts of swan meat with sugar and spices.

Staffordshire oatcakes are a crowning glory of British regional food. Soft, thin, savoury pancakes, they are made with oatmeal, flour and yeast and cooked on a griddle or 'backstone' and eaten hot. With a delicate, lacy texture and a nutty, moreish flavour, oatcakes are served filled or topped with any combination of grated cheese, tomato, onion, bacon, sausage, egg, mushrooms and baked beans. They can also be bought in packs of six or twelve to be eaten later, cold or reheated. The Derbyshire oatcake has similar ingredients but is larger and thicker.

Strong flavours are part and parcel of Midlands cuisine, from the sage added to Lincolnshire sausages to an array of umami-laden condiments. The recipe for Worcestershire Sauce is a closely guarded secret, but we know its ingredients to include fermented anchovies, brine, molasses, vinegar, tamarind, garlic, onions and spice. Fruity, spicy, sweet and sour HP Sauce was invented in Nottingham and was for many years made in Birmingham, as was its rival Daddies. Strangest of all is Marmite. The yeast extract with the powerful, love-it-or-loathe-it taste was invented in Burton-on-Trent and is still made there, using by-products from the town's famous breweries.

The 'three counties' of Herefordshire, Worcestershire and Gloucestershire are the apple and pear growing heartland of England (Worcestershire's county emblem is a pear). Industrially-produced cider, made from sugar and fruit concentrates, the kind that is often served over ice cubes, has little in common with 'real cider' made from freshly pressed apples by small Midlands producers using traditional methods.

The fruit loaf (or tea loaf) crops up throughout Britain, with subtle local variations. My favourite is Lincolnshire plumbread which manages to be simultaneously rich, light and moist, with none of the choking dryness and cloying sweetness that afflict lesser loaves. It's great energy food for cycling. Shrewsbury cake is a large, shortbread flavoured with rosewater and, though gingerbread is found everywhere in Britain, the kind from Ashbourne in Derbyshire has long been prized among visitors. Bakewell's famous Pudding is very likely the result of a kitchen accident, but that has not held it back. A rustic calorie-bomb, it is puff pastry topped with jam and a sweet filling made of egg and almond paste. The Bakewell tart is a more recent refinement of the same basic concept. Sweet steamed puddings abound, and two interesting ones are Malvern pudding, composed of apples and custard, and Lincolnshire carrot pudding, a lighter version of a traditional Christmas pudding.

Cheddar may have conquered the world, but Stilton has long been the connoisseurs' choice among British cheeses. Officially, the pungent blue-veined cheese can only be made in three counties: Nottinghamshire, Leicestershire and Derbyshire. Three of the six remaining creameries are in the Vale of Belvoir. Look out also for Stichelton from near Sherwood Forest. Made from raw milk using traditional methods, it is perhaps closer to the authentic, old-fashioned Stilton. The revival of artisanal British cheesemaking in the past few decades is nothing short of miraculous. There are too many for a comprehensive list, but Evenlode, Rollright and Harefield from Gloucestershire, Dorstone and Ragstone from Herefordshire, Berkswell from Warwickshire, and Lincolnshire Poacher are all winners in my experience.

No. 6 STAFFORDSHIRE ROLLERCOASTER

Fill your pannier with picnic fixings at the Denstone Hall Farm Shop or stop in at the café where an all-day breakfast is served on Staffordshire oatcakes. Cheddleton is the home of the Staffordshire Cheese Company and the Rambler's Retreat in Dimmings-dale serves food all day, including cream teas and the mammoth 'Lords and Ladies Afternoon Tea'.

No. 10 OVER THE EDGE

Ludlow is the gastronomic capital of Shropshire and the Welsh Marches. The route passes the Ludlow Farmshop which takes pride in sourcing 80% of its stock locally. It's a good place to pick up supplies for a picnic lunch. There are several food-oriented pubs en route, and Ludlow has a choice of great places for an evening meal.

No. 18 CANAL CITY

Panjabi Rasoi is a great value and vegetarian-friendly canteen-café at the midpoint of this ride. It is the perfect stop-off for a nourishing lunchtime thali washed down with a salted lassi.

No. 23 TO THE MANOR BORN

The gastronomic highlights of this ride are the brilliant Pickle and Pie, a small rustic café in Crick, and Squisito, an Italian butcher, cheese shop, deli and cookery school in Yelvertoft.

No. 25 HIGHER GROUND

As well as offering famous pork pies from Melton Mowbray this ride passes a couple of food-oriented country pubs. The Stag & Hounds in Burrough on the Hill is a Michelin Bib Gourmand-winning pub serving a forward-thinking menu from local producers. The Fox and Hounds in Knossington is a relaxed dining pub serving more traditional fare.

No. 26 FAT OF THE LAND

This ride is a gourmet's dream, from the 'damn fine coffee' at Café Allez! near Belvoir Castle, to Stilton cheese straight from the dairy at Colston Bassett, and local venison, bison and more from farm cafés Nice Pie and Through the Gate. Dickies Farm Dining does a memorable Sunday lunch and, for overnight stays, the Thatch in Bottesford is a cosy fine-dining restaurant with rooms.

No. 30 OUT TO LUNCH

The Cheese Shop in Louth is widely feted not just for its selection of cheese, but other delicacies that would happily grace a gourmet picnic pannier. Savoury tarts, frangipanes, cheese scones and brownies are baked on the premises daily. Around the corner is Pocklington's Bakery, where you can choose from several varieties of Lincolnshire plumbread.

BEST FOR

HISTORY

—

As the great ice sheets that once blanketed northern Europe were receding, tribes of nomadic hunter-gatherers ventured across the tundra and took shelter in the caves of a limestone ravine on what is now the Derbyshire-Nottinghamshire border. The discoveries at Creswell Crags include cave art and a rib bone engraved with the image of a horse's head that predate Stonehenge by as much as ten thousand years. They mark the beginning of the continuous inhabitation of Britain (see Ride No. 28).

The recorded history of Central England begins much later, with the Romans. They built their great military roads across the region, and built towns and villas where commerce and culture flourished. The Anglo-Saxon kings of Mercia, who made their capital at Tamworth, were a dominant force in what would later become England.

The Midlands has been at the heart of the conflicts that shaped English history: the Wars of the Roses, the Reformation, the Gunpowder Plot and the Civil War. The industrial revolution was kindled on the banks of the Severn in Shropshire and the Derwent in Derbyshire. The thinkers and

doers of the 'Midlands Enlightenment' moved England into the modern age. Birmingham grew from a Saxon village to become the workshop of the world; Stoke-on-Trent took on the ceramics industries of Asia and Europe and won. Coventry gave us the familiar diamond-shaped bicycle frame we still ride today; Nottingham exported Raleigh bikes around the globe. The past is all around us. But it only becomes history when you slow down enough to think about it. This is what makes the bicycle a perfect vehicle for time-travellers.

No. 3 SUPER OFF-PEAK

After Queen Elizabeth herself, Bess of Hardwick was the wealthiest and most powerful woman in Elizabethan England, and she wanted the world to know it. Architecturally, Hardwick Hall is a powerful statement and houses a collection of exquisite treasures from tapestries and paintings to furniture and ornaments.

No. 4 HAPPY TRAILS

Cromford has a good claim to be the birthplace of the modern factory system. The buildings that housed Richard Arkwright's water-powered cotton mills are now part of a UNESCO World Heritage Site. This ride uses former industrial routes to climb onto the high plateau of the Peak District; it returns via the quintessential estate village of Tissington, still run by its own 'lord of the manor'.

No. 6 STAFFORDSHIRE ROLLERCOASTER

Once a hive of industry, the Churnet Valley is now a haven of tranquillity, but many fragments of its past remain, from huge lime kilns to the mill complex at Cheddleton and the Earl of Shrewsbury's carriage drive.

Cheddleton Mill

Whitchurch

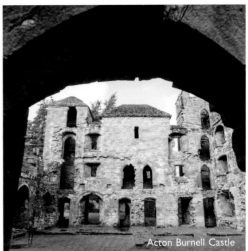
Acton Burnell Castle

No. 8 ABOUT TIME

Starting from Whitchurch, once a Roman town that became a centre for clock-making, the route passes meres and mosses that are the remnants of the last Ice Age and the canals that were the superhighways of Georgian England. With a short detour you can add the eerie shell of Moreton Corbet Castle before entering the realm of Viscount Combermere, a celebrated military commander whose connections with empire and slavery bring the controversies around Britain's history into sharp relief.

No. 11 TAKE IT TO THE BRIDGE

Few places can genuinely be said to have changed the world but Coalbrookdale is one of them. As the crucible of the industrial revolution, it was here in the Severn Gorge that Abraham Darby used coking coal to produce high-quality iron. The world's first iron bridge is a landmark in engineering and it's a thrill to cycle across it. The industrial history of the area is told in several world-class museums.

No. 16 AT THE CROSSROADS

This route follows old salt ways, Roman roads and the routes used by Welsh drovers to cross the Cotswolds. Cirencester was a major Roman settlement (complete with amphitheatre) that evolved into the splendid capital of the Cotswolds. Chedworth is one of the best-preserved Roman villas in Britain, with underfloor heating, saunas and mosaic floors.

No. 18 CANAL CITY

Cutting through the heart of the city, Birmingham's canal towpaths also show you its innards, from the locks, wharfs and warehouses of its industrial heyday to the mid-century concrete dystopia of Spaghetti Junction. In leafy Sutton Park is a 1½ -mile-long preserved section of Icknield Street, the Roman road between the Cotswolds and South Yorkshire.

No. 23 TO THE MANOR BORN

Like them or loathe them, the landed estates of the British aristocracy have shaped the countryside and their big houses are major repositories of art, culture and history. Northamptonshire has more than most counties and this ride takes in five of them, including Stanford Hall, an important site in the early history of aviation, and Althorp, the family home and final resting place of Diana, Princess of Wales. The route also passes Brixworth and its imposing 7th century church and Naseby, where Parliamentarians and Royalists fought a decisive battle in the English Civil War.

BEST FOR

ARTS & CULTURE

———

Royal Shakespeare Theatre, Stratford-upon-Avon

"The first real grip I ever got on things / Was when I learned the art of pedalling", begins Seamus Heaney's poem "Wheels Within Wheels". The connections between cycling and creativity run deep. Countless poets, artists, writers and musicians have found cycling to be a way to let the mind run free, and to gain a different perspective on the world. From Edward Elgar and Gustav Holst, to David Byrne and Patti Smith; from Alfred Jarry and Marcel Duchamp, to Grayson Perry and Ai Wei Wei; from Simone de Beauvoir and Henry Miller, to Iris Murdoch and Alan Bennett, the list could go on and on.

Riding a bicycle is also the perfect way to make a cultural journey through the landscape. The following rides all include a cultural landmark such as a gallery or museum, buildings and gardens created with an artistic vision, or a landscape with strong literary connections.

No. 4 HAPPY TRAILS

The Derbyshire folk-art tradition of well dressing dates back hundreds of years, and may even originate in pre-Christian pagan rituals. It takes place in as many as 70 towns and villages across the county, and over the border in Staffordshire. The Peak District village of Tissington is the best place to see these colourful tableaux made from flower petals, mosses, beans, seeds and small cones. The village has six wells and its ceremony takes place on Ascension Day, in May. Rides No. 1 and 2 also pass towns and villages where well dressing is still a tradition; check well-dressing.com for dates and locations.

No. 11 TAKE IT TO THE BRIDGE

The world-class museums in and around Ironbridge and Coalbrookdale are not just about industry and ingenuity, but creativity and artistry. The Tile Museum in Jackfield presents the dazzling story of the British decorative tile industry and the Footprint Gallery next door shows work by contemporary artists and makers. Just across the River Severn, the Coalport China Museum has a collection of fine chinaware made on the site between 1795 and 1926.

No. 13 I HEAR A SYMPHONY

The rolling countryside of Worcestershire, Herefordshire and Gloucestershire was a muse to the composer Edward Elgar, who was also an avid cyclist (Ride No. 12 passes the museum at his birthplace). The Malvern Hills are a major landmark in this landscape; and they loom large in its literature. The 14th century poet William Langland chose the hills as the setting for Piers Plowman. Elizabeth Barrett Browning, C. S. Lewis, J. R. R. Tolkien, W. H. Auden and Kazuo Ishiguro, too, have all taken inspiration from their shapely peaks and wooded slopes.

No. 14 ROADS LESS TRAVELLED

For a brief time just before the outbreak of the First World War, the villages around Dymock in Gloucestershire were the unlikely gathering place for a small group of writers seeking a new creative direction, a style of poetry rooted in everyday language and the natural world. Among the 'Dymock Poets' were Robert Frost, Edward Thomas and Rupert Brooke. Mostly they walked the fields and woods but Thomas is said to have composed his poem "Words" on May Hill while he was exploring the area by bike (you can sense the influence of such journeys in the final stanza).

No. 17 THIS CHARMING LAND

The material culture of England's medieval wool economy is on display in the many fine Cotswold buildings along the route, from country estates to merchants' townhouses to magnificent churches. The cultural highlight of the ride is Snowshill, a manor house that became a giant cabinet of curiosities thanks to its eccentric owner Charles Paget Wade, who also helped lay out an intimate Arts & Crafts garden (there's another Arts & Crafts garden at Cottesbrooke Hall on Ride No. 23).

No. 19 ESCAPE VELOCITY

This ride takes you from the centre of Birmingham through the fabled Forest of Arden to William Shakespeare's birthplace at Stratford-upon-Avon. It has become a place of pilgrimage for Shakespeare lovers, not just to visit historic sites associated with the Bard, but to see his plays performed by the Royal Shakespeare Company, which runs three theatres in the town.

No. 21 CUT TO THE CHASE

As a centre of the Midlands Enlightenment and the birthplace of Samuel Johnson, Lichfield was once a major intellectual hub; the small cathedral city still has a strong cultural streak. A waypoint on this ride is Abbots Bromley, whose annual 'horn dance' is among England's most famous folkloric rituals. Towards the end of the ride is Cannock Chase, a hilly expanse of woods and heath, and a mecca for ghost-hunters and other enthusiasts for paranormal experiences.

No. 29 WOLDS APART

The Victorian writer and art critic John Ruskin declared Lincoln cathedral to be "out and out the most precious piece of architecture in the British Isles". This ride heads from the ancient city out to the Lincolnshire Wolds, where Ruskin's contemporary, the poet Alfred, Lord Tennyson, was born and raised and whose landscape features heavily in his early poetry.

Snowshill Manor

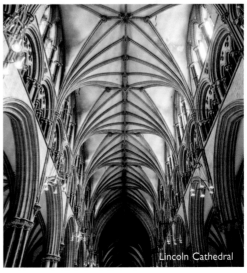

Lincoln Cathedral

BEST FOR

UPS AND DOWNS

———

Riding a bicycle down a hill is a sensation that's hard to describe but impossible to forget. It's akin to being a bird in flight: a lightness of being, a rush of speed and a feeling of carefree joy that just makes you want to smile. But there is a catch: what goes down must also go up. Riding a bicycle uphill is an acquired taste, to say the least. On the flat, the bicycle multiplies a modest amount of effort into effortless speed. On a climb, the tables are turned. Suddenly the miracle machine becomes a dead weight as you move ever slower, just trying to keep the pedals turning.

Yet there are rare moments riding uphill when the combination of physical effort and mental focus approaches a state of grace. Every rhythm, from beating heart to heaving lungs to pumping thighs and spinning pedals, comes together in a symphony of ascent. That's why climbing is so addictive and why people write entire books and websites about their favourite cycling climbs. But sometimes, when faced with a really steep climb, the best thing to do is to get off and walk. There is no shame in that. As well as giving your legs a rest, walking gives you a bit more time to appreciate your surroundings.

No. 2 HOPE SPRINGS ETERNAL

Although this ride shuns the very steepest climbs in the area such as the recently resurfaced Bamford Clough (maximum gradient 36.5%!), there's the option of taking on Winnats Pass in place of the broken road up Mam Tor. Set in a steep-sided natural bowl, Winnats is a celebrated of cycling climbs, and has been the setting for no fewer than eight National Hill Climb Championships. Motor traffic can be heavy, so it's better at quiet times and out of season.

Broken road, Mam Tor

No. 7 NATURAL HIGH

A full-fat feast of climbing starts at Bollington and doesn't really let up much after that. Long flowing descents are just as much a part of the fun. The run down Dowel Dale past the dramatic, knife-edge limestone ridges is one to remember, as is the final descent to Macclesfield, with Manchester just about visible in the distance.

No. 9 SHROPSHIRE THRILLS

This ride is defined by two big hills. A long, steady climb up the Long Mynd, followed by a white-knuckle descent down the fearsome Asterton Bank (only a true masochist would ride up it). After a brief respite comes a second ascent onto the quartzite outcrop of the Stiperstones.

Asterton Bank

Peak District

Malvern Hills

Abdon Burf

No. 10 OVER THE EDGE

This ride is lumpy rather than hilly, but it does include an entirely optional climb to the summit of Brown Clee Hill, the highest point in Shropshire. Traffic-free Abdon Burf is a brute, averaging 12% for just over a mile, but the first third is the killer: dead straight at a merciless 20-25%. The reward is fine views across the Marches and into Wales.

No. 12 SEVERN UP

The River Severn meanders through Worcestershire in very gently rolling countryside. This is why Abberley Hill comes as something of a shock, especially the top section beyond Abberley village on a steep holloway through the woods.

No. 13 I HEAR A SYMPHONY

This ride contains another optional climb, to the very top of the Malvern Hills, the highest point in Worcestershire. The climb up the traffic-free tarmac and gravel climb is less brutal than Abdon Burf and the views from the Worcestershire Beacon are just as good, down the chain of the Malverns and across the Severn Vale to the Cotswolds.

No. 17 THIS CHARMING LAND

There is no single set piece climb on this ride, rather a series of smaller ups and downs as you cut across the grain of the landscape, gradually ascending to the crest of the Cotswold escarpment at Broadway Tower and the very fast, straight descent to Chipping Campden.

BEST FOR

ROUGH STUFF

———

Off-road cycling is having a moment right now, with the emergence of gravel bikes and adventure bikes as a versatile middle ground between road bikes and mountain bikes. It is a sign that people want bikes that are capable of handling unsurfaced byways and tracks but can zip along at a good lick on the road. But off-road cycling goes back a long time. In the very earliest days of cycling, most roads were pretty rough, and many cyclists loved seeking out remote byways and upland tracks.

In the 1950s the members of the Rough Stuff Fellowship elevated riding off the beaten path to an art form; many of their exploits — on traditional steel touring bikes — are recorded in a vast archive of wonderful photography. In the 1970s, plaid-shirted Californians started racing their heavy and highly customised 'klunkers' down the hills of Marin County and went on to bequeath the world the mountain bike. Their motto "No cops, no cars, no concrete" succinctly captures the carefree appeal of riding bikes off-road.

The lesson of all this is that the kind of bike you ride is less important than having a sense of adventure, a sense of humour and not being in too much of a hurry. As Bob Harrison, an RSF founder member, liked to say, "I never go for a walk without my bike". These routes all take in sections of rough stuff, some longer than others, though there is almost always an alternative for those who prefer tarmac.

No. 4 HAPPY TRAILS

Half close your eyes while riding the Peak District's gravel rail trails and you could be on Tuscany's famous *strade bianche*. This ride also includes a few sections of unpaved farm track, of which there are many more to explore.

No. 6 STAFFORDSHIRE ROLLERCOASTER

The Churnet Valley is a real hidden gem for off-road exploring. This route is mostly on lanes but includes three off-road sections: a rough canal towpath, a good railway trail and, best of all, Lord Shrewsbury's carriage drive through the wooded valley of Dimmingsdale.

No. 15 FREEDOM OF THE FOREST

Well-known among the MTB riders, the Forest of Dean and the lower Wye valley are also gravel riding paradises, with miles of forest trails, old railways and mineral tramways, byways and bridle-ways in some of the most varied and breathtaking landscapes in England.

No. 21 CUT TO THE CHASE

Cannock Chase is a mecca for mountain biking in the West Midlands but offers plenty of good gravel trails suitable for hybrids, touring and gravel bikes. This route also makes use of canal towpaths and riverside paths as a way of avoiding busy main roads.

No. 22 GREENWOOD, GRAVEL AND GRIT

The number and variety of off-road cycleways, woodland trails and green lanes in this circuit of Charnwood Forest to the west of Loughbor-ough will come as something of a surprise. It shows that good off-road riding can be found almost anywhere.

No. 28 THE WAY THROUGH THE WOODS

Half of this route is on woodland tracks and farm bridleways through landed estates that occupy the remnants of Sherwood Forest. As ever, it is a revelation to discover just how far it is possible to travel without encountering a car.

BEST FOR

WEEKENDS AWAY

———

All the rides in this book can be done in a single day, but they are easily adaptable into weekends away or multi-day mini-tours, either by splitting a single ride over two days or by stitching two or more rides into a longer tour.

The good news is that there has never been more choice in places to stay: from tiny campsites where you can get back to nature, through camping barns and youth hostels, all the way to cosy B&Bs, historic coaching inns and boutique hotels. I have put my recommendations in each ride's listing of pubs and pit stops. These are my suggestions for multi-day tours linking two or more rides.

DERBYSHIRE DALES (RIDES No. 1, 2 & 4)

The limestone country of Derbyshire's White Peak offers a winning combination of lofty uplands, deep-cut gorges and picture-postcard villages, all connected by quiet lanes and traffic-free cycle trails. Stitching these three rides together takes in the spa town elegance of Buxton, pretty villages like Youlgreave, Tideswell and Tissington, the 'shivering mountain' of Mam Tor and the ancient stone circle at Arbor Low.

WESTERN PEAK (RIDES No. 5, 6 & 7)

Rides No. 5 and 7 are, in effect, a tour of the western side of the Peak District, from the train station at Macclesfield to the historic market town of Ashbourne and back, through some dramatic landscapes with some big hills. Take an extra day to add in Ride No. 6, exploring the lanes and gravel trails of the Churnet Valley, once a centre of Staffordshire's metal and mineral industry but now a haven of nature and tranquillity.

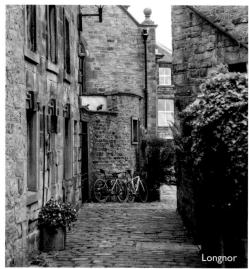
Longnor

Stow on the Wold

ELGAR COUNTRY (RIDES No. 12, 13 & 14)

These three rides cover a landscape beloved - and much cycled - by the composer Edward Elgar, from Stourport in the north to Newent in the south. There is good train access at Droitwich, Worcester, Malvern and Ledbury. The last of these is an especially handsome and historic town that makes a great base for exploring the area.

THE COTSWOLDS (RIDES No. 16 & 17)

It would be easy to spend a fortnight or more exploring the lanes and byways of the Cotswolds, but this pair of rides will make for a decent weekend. They are, in effect, a figure-of-eight with a short connecting section on National Cycle Route 48 between Farmington and Coln St Dennis. There are railway stations to the south at Kemble and to the north at Moreton-in-Marsh.

SOUTH WARWICKSHIRE (RIDES No. 19 & 20)

There is something satisfying about starting a long bike ride from a major city centre, and a real sense of achievement in breaking out through the ring of suburbs into the countryside. Starting in Birmingham, with an overnight stop in Warwick or Leamington Spa, these two rides showcase the gentle beauty of southern Warwickshire taking in iconic landmarks such as Stratford-upon-Avon,

the Grand Union Canal, the Burton Dassett Hills and the Chesterton windmill.

EAST MIDLANDS (RIDES No. 24, 25 & 26)

Though beloved by local cyclists, this area doesn't attract anywhere near the number of people from outside the East Midlands that it deserves. These three routes straddle the Vale of Belvoir, High Leicestershire, Rutland and the Rockingham Forest. It's perfect cycling country, with a dense network of narrow lanes and just enough variation in the landscape to keep it interesting without being hard work. It's also becoming a real gastronomic destination, which only adds to the appeal.

LINCOLNSHIRE (RIDES No. 29 & 30)

Lincolnshire is a big county and it takes at least two days cycling to make a dent in it. These rides are a mini-tour from Lincoln to Louth, the county's nicest town, taking in a good chunk of the Wolds, where some of the county's best cycling is to be found. Once you've made it to Louth the temptation to get to the coast will be strong, so you might want to add in an extra day's riding, perhaps to the nature reserve at Donna Nook to see the seals that gather there. For a more traditional British seaside experience head for Mablethorpe, Anderby Creek or Chapel St Leonards.

PEAK DISTRICT

No. 1

PEAK PLEASURE

From Buxton to Bakewell and back through
the limestone heart of the White Peak

———

With its hilly setting and exuberant architecture, Buxton is a match for any spa town in Britain. On a cold island far from home, the Romans must have been glad of its geothermal spring, which emerges at a steady 28 degrees centigrade. They named their settlement here *Aquae Arnemetiae*, Baths of the Goddess of the Sacred Grove. In medieval England, when the spring was dedicated to St Ann, pilgrims made the journey here for spiritual and physical healing.

The Georgian spa boom owed much to the Cavendish family of Chatsworth, near Bakewell, who built many of the town's fine buildings, including the Buxton Crescent which is modelled on the Royal Crescent in Bath. Buxton's architecture is an intoxicating mix of Georgian refinement, Victorian opulence, Romanesque and Vernacular styles as well as early examples of Arts & Crafts. There are three wellness spas in the town and you can fill your water bottles with the celebrated spring water, for free, at the spout at St Ann's Well, facing the Crescent Ⓐ.

For cyclists there are, as yet, no really pleasant ways in and out of Buxton, so the first and last miles of this ride are on roads that are busier than is ideal. Leaving the town centre on London Road, it's a steady climb to Harpur Hill, where the route follows the Pennine Cycleway onto a good traffic-free gravel track past a string of limestone quarries. The first of these is the disused Hoffman quarry Ⓑ. Now flooded, its vivid azure blue waters draw thousands of visitors, despite warnings about the toxic alkalinity of the chalky water, and the amount of rubbish — from car wrecks to dead animals — that lies beneath the surface. In a reverse tourist promotion campaign, the council periodically dyes the water black, and farmers have spread pig and cow slurry around the surrounding land.

Back onto tarmac lanes, the next section is a breathtaking balcony lane above Dovedale, which marks the boundary between Derbyshire and Staffordshire. The White Peak is so-called because of its limestone geology. The pale colour of the rock contrasts with the darker shale and gritstone found in other parts of the Peak District and known, descriptively enough, as the Dark Peak. In and around Dovedale the limestone is at its most spectacular; it's curious to think that these strangely shaped hills and ridges are the remnants of reefs and atolls in a tropical sea.

At Parsley Hay the route crosses beneath the High Peak Trail (see Ride No. 4), goes across the A515, then continues east past the Arbor Low stone circle Ⓒ. This Neolithic henge monument is among the most important prehistoric site in the region, with a wild and lonely setting high on

---

START & FINISH: Buxton • DISTANCE: 35 miles / 56km • TOTAL ASCENT: 904m
TERRAIN: Mostly lanes with 7 miles on good gravel tracks. Moderate.

Litton Mill

Headstone Viaduct

Middleton Moor. It's open all hours, and access is through private land for which the landowner charges £1 per person.

The long descent from Arbor Low reveals a gentler side of the Peak District. The lovely village of Middleton is set on the edge of a densely wooded ravine. The narrow streets of pretty Youlgreave once rang with the clatter of miners' boots, but it's now a popular base for visitors to the area. There are two good river swimming spots nearby. The first is a stone-built pool, originally used as a sheep wash — from the centre of Youlgreave follow Holywell Lane downhill, then turn left onto the riverside path Ⓓ. The second is in Lathkill Dale, with less of a detour — after crossing Conksbury Bridge, follow the footpath on the left side of the road Ⓔ.

Following a stiff climb out of Lathkill Dale, the route heads for the Monsal Trail. Built for the Midland Railway, this is among the most popular cycling and walking routes in Britain, with a winning combination of great scenery, a good surface, spectacular viaducts and atmospheric tunnels. The obvious way is to cross the River Wye at Bakewell, joining the Monsal Trail via Coombs Road Ⓕ. I prefer the more scenic option, which omits Bakewell by continuing along Crowhill Lane, crossing the Wye at Ashford-in-the-Water and joining the trail at Thornbridge.

The beautiful landscape of the Monsal Trail jars with the gruesome history of the former cotton mills at Litton and Cressbrook Ⓖ. In this sparsely populated farming area, the mill owners struggled to find workers, so they conspired with unscrupulous workhouse masters in London to traffic orphaned and pauper children into what amounted to slavery. In the early 19th century hundreds of boys and girls as young as seven were forced to work sixteen-hour days operating dangerous and noisy machinery. The children were underfed and kept in cold, bleak, over-crowded and unsanitary conditions. They were often beaten and abused. Dozens died. Truly, these were England's darkest and most satanic mills. They have since been converted into luxury flats.

Unfortunately the Monsal Trail doesn't follow the railway line all the way to Buxton. The reason is that beyond Wye Dale the line is still used to service limestone quarries. So at Miller's Dale it's necessary to continue by road, climbing through Wormhill, one of a handful of localities that claim to be the place where the last wolf in England was hunted down and killed.

There is no pleasant way into Buxton from the north-east so, until Derbyshire county council invests in some decent cycle infrastructure, it's a matter of following the least worst of the various possible routes. For now, this is probably Batham Gate Road, Waterswallows Lane and Waterswallows Road, with the option of an unsurfaced but rideable right-of-way across the golf course.

PUBS & PIT STOPS

THE ROYAL OAK, Hurdlow, SK17 9QJ (01298 83288) Just off route, a popular country pub with camping and bunk barn. Food served all day.

PEAK FEAST, Moor Lane, Youlgreave DE45 1US (01629 630000) Excellent vegetarian café for cakes, toasties, homity pies and more.

THE BULLS HEAD, Church Street, Ashford-in-the-Water DE45 1QB (01629 812931) Homely Robinsons brewery pub with a large back garden.

AISSEFORD TEA ROOM, Church Street, Ashford-in-the-Water (01629 812773) Small tearoom serving light lunches, outside seating available.

Plenty of choice in Bakewell if you go that way, including **THE GALLERY CAFÉ** in the Rutland Arms Antiques Centre, The Square DE45 1BT (07814 888251), **THE WOODYARD** Coombs Road DE45 1AQ (01629 690140) or, for Bakewell puddings, take your pick among **THE BAKEWELL PUDDING PARLOUR, BLOOMERS** and **THE OLD ORIGINAL BAKEWELL PUDDING SHOP.**

QUACKERS CAFÉ, Thornbridge Hall, Great Longstone DE45 1NZ (07771 588981) Cheery café on the Thornbridge Estate, with outside seating. Easy access from the Monsal Trail.

DALE FARM CAMPING, Moor Road, Great Longstone DE45 1UA (0333 050 3440) Just off route, a lovely farm campsite with bell tents also available. Close to the excellent Packhorse Inn in Little Longstone.

BIKE SHOP: Peak Ascent Cycles, 6 The Colonnade, Buxton SK17 6AL (01298 299011); Peakland Cycles, The Old Smithy, Milford, Bakewell DE45 1DX (01433 639853).

BIKE HIRE: Parsley Hay Bike Hire, Repair and Service Centre, SK17 0DG (01298 84493); Monsal Trail Cycle Hire Centre, Hassop Station, near Bakewell DE45 1NW (01629 810588).

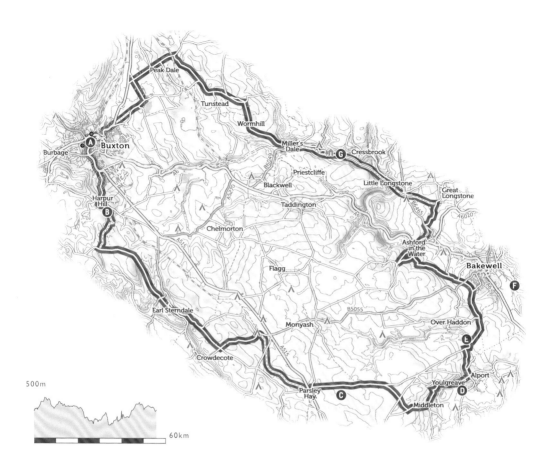

500m

60km

Monsal Trail

Monsal Head

No.2

HOPE SPRINGS ETERNAL

A short but action-packed exploration of the Hope Valley
and the limestone plateau to the south

———

Some may take issue with the inclusion of a Hope Valley route in a book about cycling in Central England. The railway running through the valley links Manchester and Sheffield, two unquestionably Northern cities. Both exert an influence on this part of the Peak District. Yet it is Derbyshire and the river Noe, which carved the valley, flows south into the Derwent and, eventually, the Trent, the great river of the East Midlands. What's more, the valley may once have been part of a line of demarcation between the kingdoms of Mercia and Northumbria. It's said that the border combined landscape features with a man-made earthwork known as Bradwell Grey Ditch. Whether you regard the Hope Valley as the Midlands or the North, it is without question a fantastic place to explore by bike, with a wealth of lanes, byways and bridleways. This ride packs an enormous amount into just over 25 miles. As a Sheffield-based friend who helped me devise the route puts it, "all killer, no filler".

From Hope, the route takes the back road to Castleton. Geologically, this is where the pale limestone of the 'White' Peak meets the darker shale and gritstone of the 'Dark' Peak. Limestone and shale are the two main components of cement, which explains why the largest cement works in the UK was built right here Ⓐ. Making cement is inherently energy and carbon-intensive, and accounts for around 8% of global carbon dioxide emissions. This single plant produces more than half of all carbon dioxide emissions in the Peak District National Park.

The area around Castleton is also known for its huge limestone caverns, several of which have been made accessible as 'show caves' with walkways, ladders, bridges, colourful lighting and even underground boat rides. Writing in 1586, William Camden described Peak Cavern or, as it was known back then, The Devil's Arse, as "one of the wonders of England" Ⓑ. It still draws the crowds to Castleton.

Overlooking Castleton is Mam Tor, Mother Hill, named on account of the continuous landslide which creates mini-hills on its eastern face. This geological instability also explains its alternative name of Shivering Hill. The road up Mam Tor, built in 1819 to replace the steep packhorse route via Winnats Pass, was repeatedly damaged and repaired before finally being abandoned in 1979. It is now a 'broken road' but still just about passable by bike Ⓒ. Winnats Pass is a fully rideable alternative and a famous cycling hill climb, though it can get busy with traffic at weekends and during the summer. The choice is yours.

Turning south at Perryfoot, you'll leave the

START & FINISH: Hope • DISTANCE: 28 miles / 45km • TOTAL ASCENT: 764m
TERRAIN: Lanes with two short off-road sections (1½ miles total) plus the Mam Tor broken road. Moderate.

Broken Road, Mam Tor

crowds far behind and set out on a sublime few miles, passing beneath the crags of Hay Dale and then descending into Tideswell. Once the capital of the medieval Royal Forest of the Peak, and a market for local farmers and industries including quarrying, lead mining and cotton and velvet mills, Tideswell is now a popular hub for visitors to the Peak District. It hosts a week-long summer festival that reaches a climax on Big Saturday when a brass band leads a torchlight procession through the streets and there is much dancing and making merry. The 14th century village church is known as 'the cathedral of the Peak'; it has some tremendous wooden carvings and stone memorials.

On the road into the village of Windmill, the route passes the well-preserved remains of the High Rake lead mine, one of the most ambitious mining projects in the Peak District Ⓓ. After centuries of mining had removed all the surface ores, an attempt was made in the 1830s to reach the ore beneath a layer of volcanic 'toadstone'. A large Cornish pumping engine was installed and, though a shaft was dug to a depth of over 220 metres, the toadstone proved too thick. The mine was closed with huge financial losses.

Just past Great Hucklow and the historic Camphill Gliding Club is the scenic highlight of the entire ride, the magnificent ridge road through the hamlet of Bretton. From here you can look south across the village of Foolow, set in a vast checkerboard of farm fields, and north across heather-clad Abney Moor. The route keeps to the high ground above Eyam, the village made famous for the selfless heroism of its inhabitants who, after an outbreak of the bubonic plague in 1665, quarantined themselves from the outside world for over a year. Mompesson's Well is one of the locations where merchants from neighbouring villages left supplies in exchange for coins dipped in vinegar for disinfection Ⓔ. Some 260 of Eyam's villagers died, between half and three-quarters of the population, but the plague stopped with them, and the rest of Derbyshire was saved.

The descent from Eyam Edge is along Sir William Hill Road. Nobody knows for sure who Sir William was, but the road has a long pedigree. It was originally a packhorse route and part of the network of saltways connecting Cheshire with South Yorkshire and the east coast, later becoming a turnpike, which probably accounts for its width and straightness. Take care not to overshoot the left turn into Sherriff Wood, above Grindleford. This is another five-star lost lane that flows beneath spreading beech trees all the way down to the valley floor at Leadmill.

From here it's uphill again, on the road to Abney, bearing right onto a corker of a twisting, grass-up-the-middle lane. There are views across the valley to Hathersage and the ramparts of Stanage Edge on the horizon. Beyond handsome Offerton Hall, the lane becomes an unsurfaced track for a brief rough-stuff coda until you emerge back into the modern world at Brough and pick up the road back to Hope.

PUBS & PIT STOPS

TILLY'S, CROSS STREET, Castleton S33 8WH (01433 620834) Decent café for breakfasts light lunches and afternoon teas.

RUSHOP HALL, Rushup Lane, Rushup SK23 0QT (01298 813323) B&B and self-catering accommodation in a grand Georgian farmstead, popular with cyclists, walkers and horse-riders.

Plenty of choice in Tideswell including **HIGH NELLY'S CAFÉ,** SK17 8LA (07906 160691) for brunch, lunch, coffee & cake, and **TINDALLS,** SK17 8NU (01928 871351) an award-winning bakery and deli.

THE ANCHOR INN, Four Lanes End, near Tideswell SK17 8RB (01298 871371) Relaxed former coaching inn, real ales and pub grub served all day.

BARREL INN, Bretton S32 5QD (01433 630856) Fabulous views from the highest pub in Derbyshire. Inside, it's oak beams, flagstone floors, open fires and lot of history. Rooms available.

BRETTON HOSTEL, Bretton S32 5QD (07792 385134) Ecologically-aware former YHA hostel set in species-rich hay meadows next door to the Barrel Inn.

YHA EYAM, Hawkhill Road, Eyam S32 5QP (03453 719 738) Hostel accommodation in a Victorian folly.

THE ANGLERS REST, Main Road, Bamford, S33 0DY (01433 659 317) Off route, but worth a detour for this stylish community pub, post office and cafe.

BIKE SHOP: Bike Garage, Unit 3, Hope Valley Garden Centre, Hope Road, Bamford, S33 0AL (01433 659345) Bike hire available.

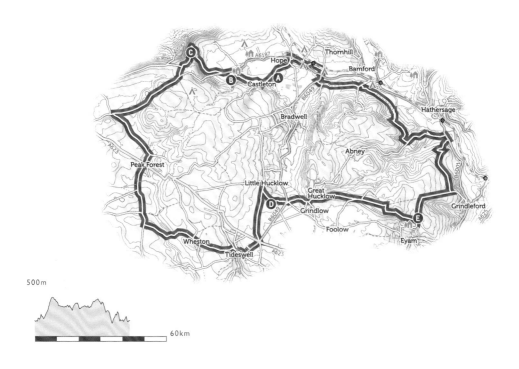

500m

60km

Hope Cement Works

No.3

SUPER OFF-PEAK

From Chesterfield's crooked spire
to the crooked lanes of Ashover parish

———

In his brilliant 1988 book *English Country Lanes: A Celebration of Travelling Slowly*, the photographer, writer and cyclist Gareth Lovett Jones proposes a new method for exploring the countryside. As an alternative to 'passing through' a linear or circular route, he argues for identifying a cohesive 'lanescape' bounded by larger roads and 'cycling along each and every lane… until there are few lanes left which he has not at some point traversed'. The parish of Ashover, between Chesterfield and Matlock, is a prime candidate for Lovett Jones' 'network system'. This ride, though it follows a traditional circular-type route, could easily be paired with a more free-form Lovett Jones type of exploration, ideally over more than one day.

The ride starts at Chesterfield railway station, a stone's throw from the church with its famously crooked spire. Folk legend says it was kicked by the Devil's hoof, after he had been badly shod by a blacksmith in Bolsover. There are other, more practical theories: that it was built during a skills shortage following the Black Death; that it was built from unseasoned timber; and, most likely, that the twist was caused by the addition of a 33-ton lead covering to the original shingle. The lead heated up faster on the sunnier south-facing side, so causing uneven expansion and contraction, and all the extra weight increased the stress on the structure.

Chesterfield stands atop a vast coalfield that extends from West Yorkshire to Nottingham. The route out of town passes the sites of a handful of old collieries, though close to nothing remains above ground. The imposing ruins of Sutton Scarsdale Hall are still very much there Ⓐ. The leading craftsmen of the day built a Baroque mansion, the costs proving too great for its owner's heirs. In the 1920s the interiors were sold off as architectural salvage. The shell is now in the care of English Heritage, although three of the original rooms can be seen in the Museum of Art in Philadelphia. From the front you can look across the valley where the M1 motorway runs, and make out the battlements of Bolsover Castle.

After picking a route through Heath, then crossing beneath the M1, it's onto the main carriage drive of another big country estate. And Hardwick Hall is not just big, it's bling. It was built for Elizabeth, Countess of Shrewsbury, better known as Bess of Hardwick. Thanks to her four canny marriages, Bess became the second richest and most powerful woman in Elizabethan England after the queen herself. Bess's wealth and status is expressed through the new Renaissance language of style, scale and symmetry rather than crude turrets and battlements. The whole thing us topped off by Bess's initials 'ES' carved in giant stone letters 16

START & FINISH: Chesterfield • DISTANCE: 37 miles / 60km • TOTAL ASCENT: 793m
TERRAIN: Mostly surfaced lanes, with a 4 mile section of gravel rail-trail. Moderate.

Old Hardwick Hall

times on the balustrades. The philosopher Thomas Hobbes was employed by the family as a tutor and secretary, and returned in later life as a friend of the family. He is buried in the church at nearby Ault Hucknall. Hardwick Hall was restored from a state of disrepair in the 1950s; it is now cared for by the National Trust (£, members free) Ⓑ. Adjacent to the big house is the shell of Hardwick Old Hall, the house where Bess was born.

Hardwick stands on the Nottinghamshire border, and just past the estate is Silverhill, the landscaped former coal mining spoil heap that is less than a metre shy of being the highest point in the whole county. There is a good gravel track to the viewpoint at the top Ⓒ. South of the hill is the Silverhill Trail, one of several old railways in the area that have been converted into cycling and walking routes, heading back into Derbyshire.

Love Lane is a charming way to arrive into Stonebroom, but the road through the former coal mining village is a little unpleasant amid the traffic, until you cross the River Amber and enter the enchanted lanescape of Ashover parish. From here, my route is just one of any number of possibilities. Get out the map and take your pick. Though it all feels very green and pleasant today, the dense network of lanes, byways and bridleways is, in part, due to Ashover's past as a local centre of lead mining, quarrying and the textile industry. The village church in Ashover contains a rare Norman font made from lead - one of just 29 in England. It survives only because, amid a skirmish in the Civil War, villagers hid it from marauding Roundhead soldiers who were looking for lead to make bullets. As the Roundheads melted down the church's leaded windows, their Royalist foes slaughtered livestock, ransacked the wine cellars of a local manor house and drank the pub dry.

From the village of Ashover, my route climbs through the hamlet of Rattle — said to have been named for the sound of the first knitting machines (the whole area was a local centre of the textile industry in the early years of mechanisation). Once up onto the high plateau to the north of Ashover, farmland gives way to the open country of Beeley Moor ⒟. This is the grouse-shooting back yard of the Chatsworth estate, and in August and September it's a purple sea of flowering heather.

From the top of the moor, it's downhill all the way to Chesterfield. There are two options for the descent to the village of Holymoorside. Most local cyclists use the fast, straight Longside Road, which takes in a bit more heather moorland. I prefer the quieter Harewood Road which follows the River Hipper through a densely wooded valley. The Hipper Valley Cycleway is a good, traffic-free route back into the town centre.

PUBS & PIT STOPS

THE HARDWICK INN, Hardwick Park S44 5QJ (01246 850245) Handsome pub and café with lots of outdoor seating, popular with cyclists. Food served all day.

THE MINERS ARMS, Oakstedge Lane, Milltown, S45 0HA (01246 590218) Popular pub-restaurant; booking advised.

THE OLD POETS' CORNER, 1 Butts Rd, Ashover S45 0EW (01246 590888) Old school village boozer, pub grub.

STAMP, Moor Road, Ashover S45 0AH (01246 591737) Post office café open all day for breakfasts, light lunches and afternoon tea. Small self-catering loft apartment available.

ANNA'S TUCK SHOP, Church Street, Ashover S45 0EW. Village shop serving home-made cakes and hot drinks.

THE BULL'S HEAD, New Road, Holymoorside S42 7EW (01246 569999) Smart dining pub with an outside terrace for an end-of-ride pint.

BIKE SHOP: Halfords, Unit 4, Netto Retail Park, 358 Sheffield Rd, Chesterfield S41 8JZ (01246 559897), J E James Cycles, Progress House, Brimington Road North, Chesterfield S41 9AP (01246 453453).

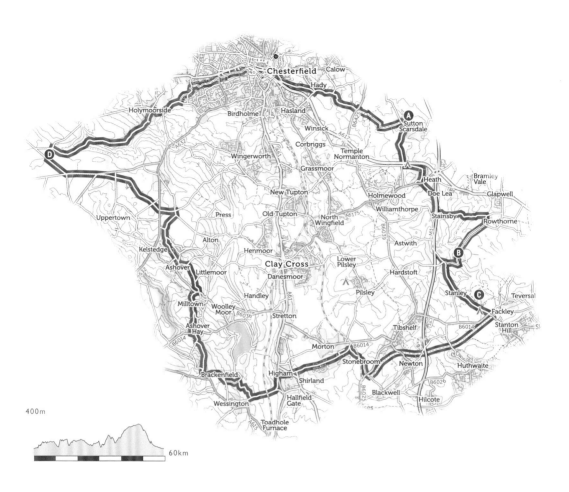

400m

60km

The Hardwick Inn, Hardwick Park

Beeley Moor

No.4

HAPPY TRAILS

Riding the railways that turbocharged Derbyshire's industrial revolution

———

Derbyshire has done more than any county in England to convert its disused railways into traffic-free greenways for cycling and walking. This route is a variation on the classic 'trails triangle' that combines two of the most popular Peak District cycle trails — the High Peak Trail and the Tissington Trail — with the traffic-free path around Carsington Water. The route starts at the railway station in Cromford, but starting at Middleton Top Ⓒ would avoid the steep climb up from the Derwent Valley and reduce the overall distance by 7 miles.

Cromford was one of the most important locations in the early years of the Industrial Revolution. It was here in 1771 that self-made inventor and entrepreneur Richard Arkwright built the world's earliest water-powered cotton spinning mill. It is regarded as the first modern factory, a system of production that would quickly wipe out traditional artisan cottage industries. Working conditions were severe. Two thirteen-hour shifts a day kept the factory in continuous production. Whole families were employed, including large numbers of children, as young as seven. Workers had a week's holiday a year, on condition that they didn't travel beyond Cromford. Arkwright made a fortune and set to building a country seat to match his elevated status. Willersley Castle can be seen from the bridge, though he died before it was completed. The mill complex is now part of the Derwent Valley Mills UNESCO World Heritage site and hosts a visitor centre, shops and two cafés Ⓐ.

From Cromford it's a stiff climb up Intake Lane to join the route of the Cromford and High Peak Railway. One of the earliest railways in Britain, it was built to carry minerals and goods between the Derwent Valley and the canal network around Manchester, as an alternative to the lengthy canal route to the south of the Pennines. Wagons were hauled up the many steep inclines by chain, and later by wire cables, wound by stationary engines. It ran until the 1960s and now lives a second life as the High Peak Trail for walking and cycling. On the way up you'll pass the National Stone Centre, an educational charity based in an old limestone quarry. It offers a short self-guided fossil and geology walking trail, and runs courses in dry stone walling and stone carving - including for absolute beginners Ⓑ.

Once onto the high plateau at Middleton Top, it's pleasant, traffic-free riding all the way towards Parsley Hay, where there's a café and bike hire shop Ⓔ. Before you get there, just off the route and accessible by a permissive footpath, is Minninglow Hill. At the top, in a wooded

---

START & FINISH: Cromford • DISTANCE: 41 miles / 67km • TOTAL ASCENT: 936m
TERRAIN: Two-thirds lanes, one-third gravel tracks and unsurfaced byways Moderate to Challenging.

Cromford Incline

High Peak Trail

clearing, is the largest Neolithic chambered tomb in Derbyshire and two Bronze Age bowl barrows Ⓓ. A little further along, the route passes the Friden brickworks, a major local employer for over a century, which specialises in making heat-resistant bricks for blast furnaces, glass making and other high temperature applications. The critical ingredient is silica, which for decades was quarried from local deposits, though now it is imported.

Two miles past Parsley Hay, the route leaves the High Peak Trail for an interlude of splendid gated roads, initially along Dovedale, then through Hartington. Once a local centre for the mining of ironstone, lead and limestone, Hartington is also known for its cheesemaking: its creamery is the only one in the county where Stilton is made (by law Stilton can only be made in Derbyshire, Nottinghamshire or Leicestershire).

From Hartington, a classic Peak District farm track leads to Biggin, where the route picks up another ex-railway line cycleway, the Tissington Trail. It's worth a short deviation from the most direct route to visit the pretty estate village of Tissington Ⓕ. The current lord of the manor is the amiable Sir Richard FitzHerbert, who inherited unexpectedly from his uncle and can often be seen lending a hand at the bustling cycling-friendly café opposite the church, as well as giving regular tours of the manor house. In 2007 Tissington Hall was among several historic houses to draw attention to its involvement in the slave trade and the wealth it derived from sugar plantations in the Caribbean. Tissington is a great place to witness the Peak District folk custom of 'Well Dressing'. Each year on Ascension Day (mid to late May) the village's six wells are bedecked with colourful and elaborate displays of flower petals, leaves and seeds. The tradition, dating back centuries, was originally an act of thanksgiving for the purity and constancy of the water supply. It may have evolved from a pagan ritual, or from the time of the Black Death, which killed between a third and a half of Britain's population in 1348-49.

From Tissington it's rolling lanes via Bradbourne to Carsington Water Ⓖ, a reservoir ringed by a shared use cycling and walking path, followed by one last climb back to the High Peak Trail, and the return to Middleton Top. If you've ridden up from Cromford, the way back follows the same route - take care as it's steep and the surface is loose in places.

PUBS & PIT STOPS

BLUE LAGOON CAFÉ, Porter Lane, Bolehill DE4 4LS (01629 825537) Airy café serving breakfasts and light lunches, part of the National Stone Centre.

MININGLOW MEADOWS CAMPING, Near Pikehall, DE4 2PR (07544 771805) Chilled out campsite on the High Peak Trail with hot showers, composting toilets and a snack shop.

THE ROYAL OAK, Hurdlow, SK17 9QJ (01298 83288) Popular country pub with camping and bunk barn. Food served all day.

BANK TOP FARM, Wallpit Lane, Hartington SK17 0AD (01298 84205) Farm B&B in lovely Dovedale, half a mile from Hartington.

Plenty of choice in Hartington including **HARTINGTON FARM SHOP AND CAFÉ** (01298 84496) for food and drinks, **THE OLD CHEESE SHOP** (01928 84935) for local cheese, the charming **PARSONS HOUSE B&B** (01298 84801) and **YHA HARTINGTON HALL** youth hostel in a 17th century manor house with camping and glamping (0345 371 9740).

BIGGIN HALL, Biggin SK17 0DH (01298 84451) Small and welcoming country house hotel.

WATERLOO INN, Biggin SK17 0DH (01298 84284) Friendly inn serving pub grub. Camping and glamping available.

HERBERT'S TEAROOMS, The Green, Tissington DE6 1RA (01335 350501) Justly popular bike-friendly café on the village green.

THE PUDDING ROOM, near Carsington Water DE6 1NQ (01629 540413) Just off route, an award-winning bakery with a tiny campsite, tearoom and local produce shop.

SCARTHIN BOOKS, The Promenade, Cromford DE4 3QF (01629 823272) Secret vegetarian café inside a quirky bookshop.

BIKE HIRE: Middleton Top Cycle Hire, DE4 4LS (01629 533294), Parsley Hay Bike Hire, Repair and Service Centre, SK17 0DG (01298 84493).

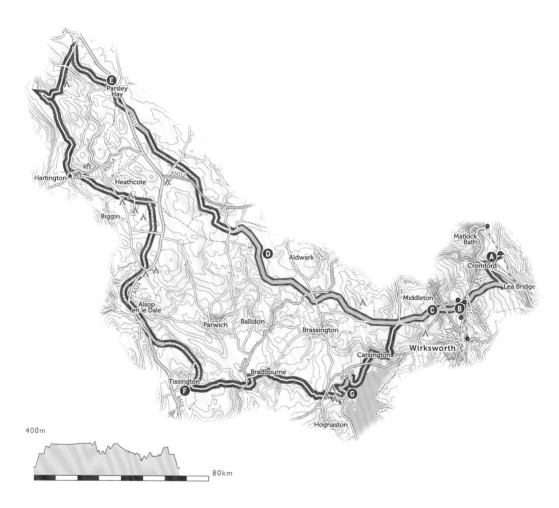

400m

80km

Hartington

Tissington

No.5

MANIFOLD DESTINY

A circuit of the southern tip of the Pennines taking in
a celebrated traffic-free cycleway and the serenity of Ilam Park

---

The very southern end of the Peak District is cut through by two rivers, the Dove and the Manifold. Each river has, year by year, cut a gorge so deep and so steep that they have largely escaped the intrusion of roads. Large parts of Dovedale can only be visited on foot, and are all the better for it. The gorges of the Manifold and its tributary, the Hamps, are tailor-made for cycling thanks to a disused railway converted to a wonderful cycling and walking trail. While the Manifold Way is the centrepiece, my route packs in much more besides.

It starts in Ashbourne, a lively market town that has more pubs than is usual for a town of its size. This may explain how the town has come to host the world's oldest, largest, longest and rowdiest game of football. More akin to a good-natured riot than a sporting fixture, the Royal Shrovetide Football Match is played annually over two days on Shrove Tuesday and Ash Wednesday, maintaining a tradition that goes back at least to the 1100s. The ball is rarely kicked; instead, it is moved through the town in a series of giant rugby scrums, made up of dozens if not hundreds of people. The goalposts are three miles apart, in villages on either side of the town, and there is no limit to the number of players on each team.

Ashbourne does have a more genteel side, with its market square and a wealth of Tudor and Georgian buildings. The church contains some of Derbyshire's best monuments, carvings and stained glass; the Victorian writer George Eliot reckoned it possessed "the finest single spire in England". Her first novel, *Adam Bede*, is set in the area, with Ashbourne appearing as Oakbourne. Several other local places and characters are recognisable.

One bad aspect of Ashbourne is its busy roads and the amount, and speed, of motor traffic. The first mile of the route is a grin-and-bear-it affair until you reach Hanging Bridge and turn left onto Watery Lane, following the River Dove as it meanders down towards the Trent. Four miles further on, there are more outstanding medieval tombs and stained glass at Norbury church Ⓐ. Crossing the river into Ellastone, the ride then follows NCR 549 north into the Weaver Hills. These limestone hills are the southernmost tip of the Pennines, the spine of England, which extends north all the way to the River Tyne.

A mile past Stanton, it's worth leaving the bike at the parking area of the Thorswood Nature Reserve, and walking up through the wildflower-rich grassland to the top Ⓑ. Depending on the time of year you may see wild thyme, salad burnet, cowslips, purple orchids, moonwort and mountain pansy. On the summit are prehistoric burial mounds, the remains of lead mines, and some huge

---

START & FINISH: Ashbourne • DISTANCE: 32 miles / 52km • TOTAL ASCENT: 783m
TERRAIN: Lanes and tarmac cycleways, two short sections of unsurfaced byway
and one short section of A-road (with footway). Moderate.

Thor's Cave

views across the surrounding landscape. Then it's a fast descent to the start of the Manifold Way, just outside Waterhouses Ⓒ. Opened in 1937, this was Britain's first 'rail trail'. It set a model for converting disused railway lines to cycling and walking routes. The original railway, a single-track narrow-gauge line that mostly transported milk from local farms, ran for less than thirty years, but was beautifully built into the tricky terrain of a steep-sided gorge. It follows the River Hamps downstream to its confluence with the River Manifold and then traces that river upstream. There are caves, crags, cliffs and caverns everywhere, but the one on all the postcards is Thor's Cave. A ten-metre-high archway on a high crag, it is clearly visible from the valley floor, 80 metres below. Archeologists have shown it was occupied from the Stone Age right through to Roman times and it's now a popular site for rock climbers. There is a stepped path to the cave from the cycle trail Ⓓ.

Much of the peace and tranquillity of the trail is down to the absence of motor vehicles.

However, the road does briefly reappear at the National Trust café and visitor centre at Wetton Mill Ⓔ. Here I prefer to switch banks onto a good farm track on the eastern side of the river, before re-joining the old railway line at Ecton Bridge. The northern terminus of the railway was at Hulme End; the station buildings now house a small museum, café and a cycle hire point Ⓕ. From here it's a long and somewhat relentless climb up to the ridgeway between the Manifold Valley and Dovedale, before climbing to the high point of the ride on Ilam Moor and another descent back into the Manifold Valley.

"Ilam has grandeur, tempered with softness," wrote Samuel Johnson after a visit in 1774. "The walker congratulates his own arrival at the place, and is grieved to think he must ever leave it." The same could be said for the cyclist and I recommend stopping for a proper look around. Ilam Hall is a grand manor house that, like so many in the decades after the first world war, had fallen into disrepair. It was saved from demolition by the self-raising flour magnate Sir Robert McDougall.

He gave it to the National Trust on the condition that it be run as a youth hostel, as it still is. The house is surrounded by Italianate gardens and parkland on the banks of the River Manifold Ⓖ. The nearby church contains a Saxon font and the medieval shrine tomb of St Bertram of Stafford, a Mercian saint. It remains a place of pilgrimage.

With no road beside the river, it's one final climb up to Blore, then a last descent to the bridge at Mapleton, where there's a good end-of-ride swim spot accessible via the footpath on the riverbank Ⓗ. The last two miles back to Ashbourne are aided by the railway tunnel at the beginning of the Tissington Trail.

PUBS & PIT STOPS

Plenty of choice in Ashbourne including **THE TUNNEL CAFÉ** 43 Church Street DE6 1AJ (01335 664069), **ST JOHN STREET CAFÉ**, 50 St. John Street DE6 1GH (01335 347425), and the **GEORGE & DRAGON**, 43 Market Place, DE6 1EU (01335 343199) a good pub with reasonably priced B&B.

MANIFOLD VALLEY CAMPSITE, Dale Farm DE6 2AG (07534 720903) Spacious camping field in a fabulous location near Wetton Mill.

WETTON MILL, Manifold Trail DE6 2AG (01298 84838) Former watermill, now a National Trust tearoom and picnic spot. Accommodation available.

THE MANIFOLD INN, Hulme End SK17 0EX (01298 84537) Large former coaching inn with rooms for overnight stays.

HULME END CAMPSITE, Hulme End SK17 0EX (07800 659985) Spacious village campsite behind the Manifold Inn.

TEA JUNCTION, Hulme End SK17 0EZ (01298 687368) Tea room at the Manifold Way Visitor Centre serving breakfasts and light snacks.

ALSTONEFIELD CAMPING BARN, Gateham Grange, Alstonefield DE6 2FT (01335 310349) Back-to-basics bunkhouse / bothy surrounded by hay meadows.

OLD SCHOOL TEA ROOM, Village Hall, Carr Lane, Wetton DE6 2AF (07801 683546) Homemade cakes and more in this village institution, plenty of outside seating.

THE WATTS RUSSELL ARMS, Hope DE6 2GD (01335 310126) Just off-route, a superb country pub serving beer, lager and cider all produced within 25 miles.

STANSHOPE HALL, Stanshope DE6 2AD (01335 310278) Much loved B&B in an elegant and imposing country house with unusual fresco interiors.

YHA ILAM HALL, Ilam DE6 2AZ (0345 371 9023) Youth hostel accommodation in an elegant manor house set in Italianate gardens.

THE OLD DOG, Spend Lane, Thorpe DE6 2AT (01335 350 990) 1½ miles off-route, north of Mapleton, a hip village pub serving gourmet sandwiches, burgers and salad bowls. Closed in winter.

BIKE SHOP: The Bike Barn, The Stables, Wellington Yard, Ashbourne DE6 1GH (01335 300708).

BIKE HIRE: Ashbourne Bike Hire, Repair and Service Centre, Mappleton Rd, Ashbourne DE6 2AA (01335 343156), Brown End Farm Cycle Hire, near Waterhouses ST10 3JR (07920 855340).

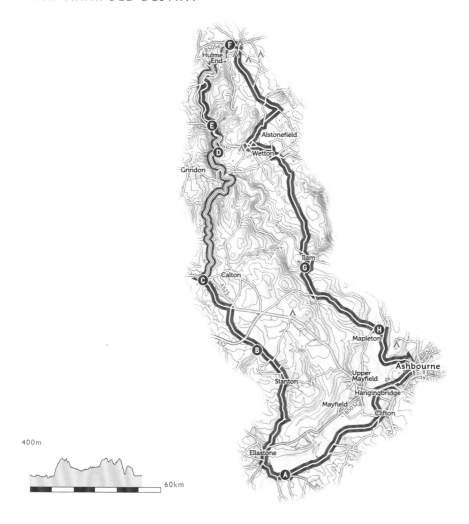

400m

60km

Ilam church

The Watts Russell Arms

Ilam park

Thorswood Nature Reserve

No.6

STAFFORDSHIRE ROLLERCOASTER

Thrills – but hopefully no spills – on the lanes,
tracks and trails of the Churnet Valley

———

Wedged between Stoke-on-Trent and the Peak District, the Churnet Valley is one of Staffordshire's hidden gems. This might seem an odd thing to say about somewhere that's home to the second most popular tourist attraction in Britain. More than two million people pass through the gates of Alton Towers each year to experience white-knuckle rides like Nemesis, The Smiler and The Wicker Man. A bike ride here might not deliver the same intense dose of pure adrenaline but it delivers a surprising variety of constantly changing landscapes and the sense of journeying back through time in this fascinating, and often overlooked, corner of the West Midlands.

The calm of the Churnet Valley owes much to the fact that it is too narrow to accommodate a road along the valley floor, though the Victorians did squeeze in a railway. In between flat sections of canal towpath and old railway line, the ride includes a fair bit of climbing up out of the valley and freewheeling back down.

The route starts in Denstone. If coming by train, the nearest station is at Uttoxeter and the best way to ride up is on the back lanes via Stramshall and Stubwood. From Denstone, the route sets out north towards Ellastone, turning west on a densely wooded lane that skirts between the grounds of two country estates. On the left, Alton Towers, once a country seat of the Earls of Shrewsbury, who built a grand Victorian stately home complete with elaborate formal gardens which included a miniature Stonehenge, Chinese pagodas and a Swiss cottage occupied by a blind Welsh harpist employed to play music around the grounds. On the right is the grounds of Wootton Lodge, a Jacobean treasure house where French philosopher Jean-Jacques Rousseau stayed while on the run in the 1760s. It was briefly, during the 1930s, the home of British Fascist leader Oswald Mosley and his wife Diana Mitford. It was later bought by J. C. Bamford, who founded the company that makes the bright yellow diggers that bear his initials, JCB (the company's global headquarters is on a huge purpose-built campus at nearby Rocester). For a closer look at the house, there is a public footpath accessible through a well-hidden gap in the stone wall two hundred yards beyond the main entrance to the estate Ⓐ.

The route descends from Farley to Oakamoor, once the centre of metal-making industries in the Churnet Valley that began over a thousand years ago and continued well into the 20th century; Oakamoor supplied the copper wire used in the first ever transatlantic telegraph cable. Local supplies of iron ore, charcoal, coal and copper, together with a reliable source of water power

———

START & FINISH: Denstone • DISTANCE: 31 miles / 49km • TOTAL ASCENT: 757m
TERRAIN: Lanes with 11 miles of unsurfaced canal towpath, forest track
and gravel rail-trail. Moderate to Challenging.

Churnet Valley Railway Path

from the River Churnet and its tributaries, provided all of the essential resources required to process metals within a small geographical area. Lime was an essential ingredient in the smelting process: both here and further on at Consall Forge you can still see the massive kilns used to convert locally quarried limestone into quick lime.

The climb up Carr Bank is a chance to test your climbing legs. After crossing the A52, a lane continues through neatly-walled hay meadows, beneath the ridge line of Ipstones Edge. From the village of Ipstones it's mostly downhill back to the river at Cheddleton. Here, at the old Flint Mill complex, you can get a sense of what life might have been like a hundred or more years ago, as narrowboats laden with minerals bound for the potteries of Stoke-on-Trent plied the

valley Ⓑ. There are records of a mill here as far back as 1253; grains were milled here throughout the medieval era. In the late 1700s the mill was converted to grind flint for the pottery industry in Stoke-on-Trent, including for Josiah Wedgwood's famous Jasperware.

From Cheddleton the canal towpaths continue on to Leek and Stoke-on-Trent, but my route turns back for the return journey to Denstone. The canal towpath can be a little muddy under wheel, but it gets better the further along you go. It's lovely section of the ride, and the steam trains which run up and down the heritage railway line only add to the sensation of travelling back in time. One thing that has improved since the area's industrial heyday is the water quality of the river, once among the most polluted in Europe, with dye works upstream in Leek and the copper works in Oakamoor discharging a toxic cocktail into the river. As the river has recovered, salmon have been successfully reintroduced and there are plans for more 'rewilding' and natural flood management.

The canal towpath comes to an end at Froghall where you can still see the derelict site of the vast wireworks that closed in 2014 ©. From here the route heads uphill once again, on the A521 to Kingsley Holt, but soon onto quieter lanes with cracking views of the rolling, wooded countryside. It's then into the trees for a sublime descent down the Dimmingsdale Valley on a carriage drive built by the Earls of Shrewsbury, who treated the whole valley as an extension of their gardens at Alton Towers. It is a ride to savour at any time of year, but is especially lovely at bluebell time in late spring and among the falling leaves of autumn ⑩.

Back once again at the river, it's a fairly swift return to Denstone along the old railway line, now a walking and cycling route.

PUBS & PIT STOPS

DENSTONE HALL FARM SHOP AND CAFÉ, Main Road, Denstone ST14 5HF (01889 590050) Large well-stocked farm shop, deli with garden café.

THE LAURELS B&B, STAR BANK, Oakamoor ST10 3DF (01538 702629) Cycling-friendly accommodation.

MANOR HOUSE FARM, Quixhill Lane, Prestwood ST14 5DD (01889 590415) Comfortable B&B in a Jacobean farmhouse. Next door is the Farm on the Hill (07597 841939) Eco-campsite with private pitches set amongst woodland and wildflower meadows.

THE CRICKETERS ARMS, The Square, Oakamoor ST10 3AB (01538 702548) Riverside freehouse.

YEW TREE INN, 3 Church Lane, Cauldon ST10 3EJ (01538 309876) 1½ miles off-route, but this eccentric Aladdin's cave of a pub is well worth a detour. Real ales, hearty food.

THE BOAT INN, Basford Bridge Lane, Cheddleton ST13 7EQ (01538 360521). Friendly pub right by the canal.

CHEDDLETON OLD SCHOOL TEA ROOMS, Hollow Lane, Cheddleton ST13 7HP (01538 528942) Teas, cakes and light meals in an old schoolhouse; outside seating available.

BLACK LION INN, Consall Forge ST9 0AJ (01782 550294) Traditional canal-side pub with a lovely car-free setting, real ales, good pub fayre.

RAMBLERS RETREAT, Dimmingsdale ST10 4BU (01538 702730) Large, popular family-run tearoom, plenty of outside seating.

BIKE HIRE: Churnet Valley Cycle Hire, Manor House Farm, Quixhill Lane, Prestwood ST14 5DD (07590 258516) Bike hire and mobile repair service.

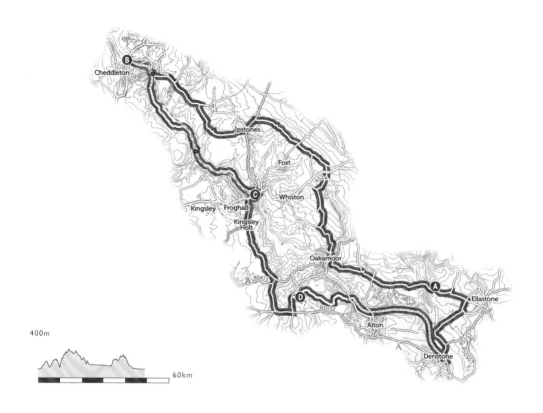

400m

60km

Cheddleton Mill

No.7

NATURAL HIGH

A big day out in the hills of the Staffordshire side of the Peak District

———

The western lobe of the Peak District is much less visited than the popular tourist destinations across the border in Derbyshire, and that makes it all the better for exploring by bike. With 1,400m vertical metres of climbing squeezed into 43 miles, this is a demanding ride. By the end it will feel even bigger than those statistics alone would imply. Maybe because it takes in such wild and lonely roads; maybe because the landscape is just so varied and so relentlessly scenic.

From the railway station in Macclesfield, the first miles are efficient, tranquil and traffic-free, on an old railway line, then switching to the canal to pick a way through Bollington. Once a rural backwater with a couple of water-powered corn and paper mills, Bollington mushroomed into a major centre of cotton spinning, with over twenty mills in operation between 1760 and 1950. The route passes the towering glass and stone frontage of Clarence Mill Ⓐ. Built for spinning high grade sea island cotton into lace, it is now converted to residential flats.

Here the climbing begins. After a couple of short, sharp efforts to reach the gritstone outcrops at Oldgate Nick, it's a fast descent to the Erwood Reservoir in the Goyt Valley. The narrow lane up Goyt's Clough is one-way (southbound). With its wooded brooks, bluebells in spring and flowering heather in late summer it is a very special road to ride. Hidden away in the woods are the ruins of Errwood Hall, a once magnificent country house built by a wealthy Manchester industrialist. The best way to get there is to take the sharp right turn onto a rideable forest track about half a mile past the Errwood Hall car park Ⓑ. It has a certain Ozymandias / 'all things must pass' allure.

At the top of the climb the modern world briefly comes roaring back in the form of the busy A-roads from Buxton, which carry a long train of lorries and cars snaking their way across the bleak moors. The lane across Axe Edge Moor, between the A54 and the A53, comes within a few hundred metres of Cheeks Hill, the highest point in Staffordshire, at 520m above sea level Ⓒ. From this high point comes a magnificent lane, descending through the dry valley of Dowel Dale and passing between the jagged limestone peaks of Parkhouse Hill and Chrome Hill. Both hills are reef knolls, the remains of coral atolls, from a time when all this land lay beneath warm tropical seas. Chrome Hill is also known as the Dragon's Back, and it's obvious why the name has stuck. Both hills are known to exhibit a rare 'double sunset' where the sun sets over the top of the hill only to re-emerge and set for a second and final time at the foot of the hill. Chrome Hill's double sunset occurs around the

START & FINISH: Macclesfield • DISTANCE: 44 miles / 70km • TOTAL ASCENT: 1412m
TERRAIN: Lanes and a short section of traffic-free cycleway. Very challenging.

summer solstice when viewed from Glutton Bridge Ⓓ, while the double sunset at Parkhouse Hill can be witnessed in late March, early April and September, from nearby Glutton Grange Farm.

It's a drag of a climb on the B5053 up to Longnor, but the village is a good spot to stop for a bite and refresh the legs. The lane south of Longnor is another corker, tracing the contours above Dovedale before rounding the corner and descending into the Manifold Valley at Hulme End, where the route meets the northernmost point of Ride No. 5. From a little way past Hulme End, another long climb begins, on the lonely lane up the Warslow Brook, through Lower and Upper Elkstone. A remote corner of the Peak, electric power and mains water did not reach here until the 1960s. The top of the climb is a long ridge of high moorland known, descriptively enough, as Morridge (moor ridge). It's another magnifi-

cent road to ride, especially in August and early September when the heather is in flower.

The jagged ramparts of Ramshaw Rocks, Hen Cloud and The Roaches mark the western edge of the Peak District. These outcrops of grippy gritstone are a mecca for rock climbers. They were also, remarkably, home to a community of wallabies after a small collection of exotic animals was released from a private zoo at Roaches Hall in the 1940s. The llamas, emus, marmots, ibex and a Himalayan yak didn't last long but the wallabies survived, increasing in number to as many as fifty. The last confirmed sighting was in 2009, and it is thought the last known pair, a female and her joey, perished in the severe winter of 2010.

From this high point, it feels like it ought to be downhill all the way back to Macclesfield. For the most part it is, but there are a couple of short sharp climbs out of wooded dingles that will be a test for tired legs. On the way down Ridge Hill (400m before the Hanging Gate Inn) is a wayside stone cross that has stood here for hundreds of years, guiding wayfarers to and from the high moor Ⓔ.

Look north and you can see Manchester in the distance, and Macclesfield closer by. Some believe the cross dates back to prehistoric times, and that it served as a plague stone, where supplies of food were left for afflicted villages in self-isolation. More recently an Ordnance Survey benchmark has been carved, marking 1,250 feet above sea level. From here it really is downhill all the way.

PUBS & PIT STOPS

LONGNOR FISH & CHIP SHOP, Market Place, Longnor SK17 0NT (01298 83317) Arguably the best chippy in the Peak District, open lunchtimes and early evening.

COBBLES COFFEE SHOP, Market Place, Longnor SK17 0NT (01298 83166) Old-fashioned café for breakfasts, baps, oat cakes and more.

THE STAFFORDSHIRE KNOT, Sheen, SK17 0ET (01298 84329) A real gem of a rural pub serving excellent food.

THE MANIFOLD INN, Hulme End SK17 0EX (01298 84537) Large former coaching inn with rooms for overnight stays.

HULME END CAMPSITE, Hulme End SK17 0EX (07800 659985) Spacious village campsite behind the Manifold Inn.

TEA JUNCTION, Hulme End SK17 0EZ (01298 687368) Tea room at the Manifold Way Visitor Centre serving breakfasts and light snacks.

THE WINKING MAN, Buxton Road, Upper Hulme ST13 8UH (01538 300361) No-frills pub on the windswept ridge — a haven when the weather's bad. Pub grub.

ROSE AND CROWN INN, Buxton Road, Allgreave SK11 0BJ (01260 227232) Traditional country inn with rooms for overnight stays.

HANGING GATE INN, Meg Lane, Higher Sutton SK11 0NG (01260 253325) Brilliant old drovers' inn with sensational views, perfect for an end-of-ride pint.

BIKE SHOP: Mac Cycles, 7 Jordangate, Macclesfield SK10 1EE (01625 400141), Peak Cyclesport, Grosvenor Centre, Macclesfield SK11 6AR (01625 426333).

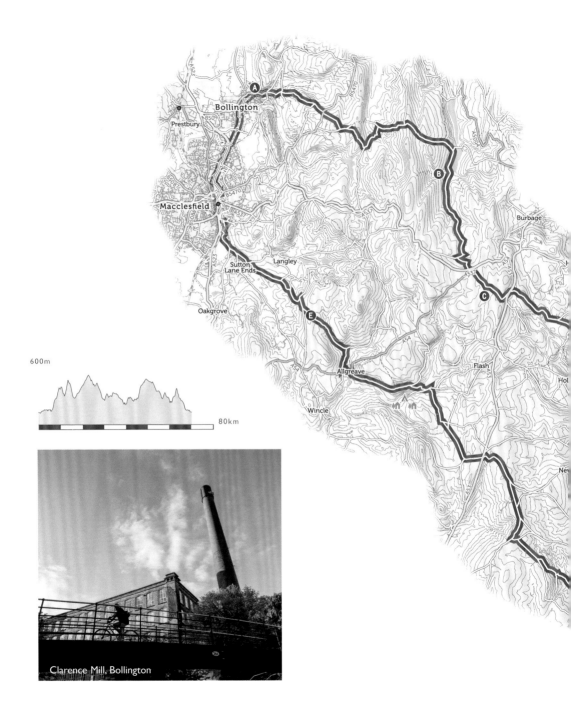

Clarence Mill, Bollington

Longnor

SHROPSHIRE & WORCESTERSHIRE

No.8

ABOUT TIME

A gentle spin around the farm lanes of the Shropshire and Cheshire border

———

Whitchurch is famous for its clocks or, more specifically, the large outdoor 'turret clocks' made by the Joyce family, who started in the clock business in 1690. Clocks emblazoned with the words 'Joyce of Whitchurch' tell the time in iconic locations around the world, from Shanghai and Sydney to Cape Town and Vancouver. Station clocks were a speciality, including what is probably the best-loved station clock in the history of cinema, on Carnforth station in Lancashire, where David Lean's *Brief Encounter* was filmed. Whitchurch is an apt place for craftsmen dealing in the passage of time, as the town has a lot of the stuff, having been in continuous occupation at least since Roman times, when it was known as *Mediolanum*. Artefacts from the town's history are on display in the heritage centre but it's equally pleasurable to play the flaneur and wander the Georgian streets and passageways.

This route captures the flavours of north Shropshire and south Cheshire, a low-lying landscape of meres, mosses and outcrops of sandstone. It is fertile land, with a strong tradition of dairy farming. Whitchurch's cheese fair was for decades the largest market for Cheshire cheese, among the oldest named cheeses in Britain. Cheshire, and the more modern Shropshire Blue, are still produced locally at the Belton dairy.

The route begins heading south out of Whitchurch towards the Llangollen canal, where it makes the briefest of forays across the border into Wales before joining the canal towpath. To the west of canal is an exceptionally rare landscape ecosystem known as a 'raised bog'. Formed from the residue of glacial lakes, the expanses of peat act like a sponge, soaking up rainwater and creating ideal conditions for acid-loving bog-mosses, cotton grasses, heather, asphodel and deer-grass. Much depleted by industrial peat extraction for use in horticulture, Fenn's Moss and Whixall Moss are now managed as nature reserves. 1,700 species of insects and other creepy crawlies have been recorded, a third of them moths. For a good view of the reserve, climb the 5m viewing platform that is a short walk from Morris' Bridge (a Grade II listed bascule bridge across the canal) Ⓐ.

The quietest of country lanes lead through Dobson's Bridge to the small market town of Wem. Its curious name derives from 'wamm', the Old English word for marsh. Beyond Wem the landscape, and indeed the lanescape, get ever more interesting. The village of Lee Brockhurst is at the southern end of a wooded sandstone ridge that, for a time, was among the most visited landscapes in Britain Ⓑ. Starting in the early 1700s, the Hawkstone estate was developed to include

START & FINISH: Whitchurch • DISTANCE: 43 miles / 69km • TOTAL ASCENT: 448m
TERRAIN: Lanes and 2 miles of unsurfaced canal towpath and rural byway. Easy.

Whitchurch

gullies, caves, tunnels, towers, bridges and assorted follies, exactly what appealed to the current tastes for the 'sublime and picturesque'. Samuel Johnson visited in 1774 and remarked on "the extent of its prospects, the awfulness of its shades, the horrors of its precipices, the verdure of its hollows and the loftiness of its rocks". The estate eventually bankrupted the Hill family; the park is now being run as a commercial visitor attraction. The route follows lanes and byways around the southern edge of the ridge with a view up to the wooded remains of an Iron Age hill fort.

From Lee Brockhurst a good green lane crosses the hill to the River Roden at Papermill Bridge. If there ever was a paper mill here, it's long gone. Another green lane heads up Papermill Bank and back onto the tarmac lanes. From here there's an option of a detour via Stanton upon Hine Heath to the ruins of Moreton Corbet Castle ©. Free to enter, the site contains the ruins of the stone castle from the 1200s and a grand Italianate extension built around 350 years later. It's an extra 5 miles, but well worth it if you have time.

After crossing the sandstone ridge of the Hawkstone estate, farm lanes lead through Darliston to a crossing point of the A41. Once a year this otherwise unremarkable A-road becomes part of the course of one of the most gruelling events in the British cycle racing calendar: the Mersey Roads 24-hour time trial. The format is simple: ride as far as you can in 24 hours. The current men's record is 544.32 miles and the women's record is 490.28 miles.

If time is tight, there is a direct route back to Whitchurch on the lane from Ightfield, passing the excellent White Lion pub, but I recommend continuing northwards and making a brief foray into Cheshire. These last miles are, in essence, a loop around Combermere Park, once a medieval monastery that, following the Reformation, became the country seat of the wealthy Cotton family.

The family's most famous son was Stapleton Cotton, the First Viscount Combermere. Born in 1773, Cotton rose from junior officer to field marshall, fighting in Britain's many wars with France and as a colonial enforcer. In India he masterminded the storming and capture of the fortress of Bharatpur on behalf of the East India Company. He was Governor of Barbados, and is known to have owned plantations and at least 420 enslaved people. A celebrity in his lifetime — huge crowds witnessed the unveiling of his statue in Chester and the village pub in Aston is still named after his greatest military success — the passage of time has cast Combermere and the colonial era he represents in a different light today. Black Lives Matter activists in Chester have called for his statue there to be removed to a museum. Halfway between Aston and Whitchurch, the route passes a field where an obelisk was erected in his memory ⒟. It is accessible by footpath. When I visited, the base of the obelisk had received a good splattering from a tractor out muck spreading, but I was able to climb the stairs to a room at the top and take in the view.

PUBS & PIT STOPS

BENJAMIN'S DELI & CAFÉ, 3 High St, Whitchurch SY13 1AW (01948 664726) Coffee and picnic fixings.

PERCY'S, Watergate Street, Whitchurch SY13 1DW (07773 034749) Unique circus-themed curiosity café.

ETZIO, 58-60 High Street, Whitchurch SY13 1BB (01948 662248) Top-notch Italian for a post-ride feast. Booking essential.

REUBEN'S BAR AND BBQ, 7 Pepper Street, Whitchurch SY13 1BG (01948 258030) Burgers, BBQ and more.

WEM TOWN HALL CAFÉ, High Street Wem SY4 5DG (01939 238270) Popular community café.

MAYPOLE COURT, 8 Maypole Court Wem SY4 5AA (01939 235802) This café-bistro is a favourite with local cyclists for coffee stops and light bites.

THE HUNGRY FROG, West Midlands Shooting Ground, Hopton TF9 3LH Bright café on a shooting range serving the usual classics plus some unexpected Asian-inspired dishes. Wed-Sat.

THE WHITE LION COMMUNITY INN, Ash Magna SY13 4DR (01948 663153) 1½ miles off-route (on the road from Ightfield to Whitchurch) but well worth the detour or short cut. Community owned pub serving hearty and great value food.

BHURTPORE INN, Wrenbury Road, Aston CW5 8DQ (01270 780917) CAMRA-award winning freehouse in the heart of the community and hosts an annual beer festival. Food served.

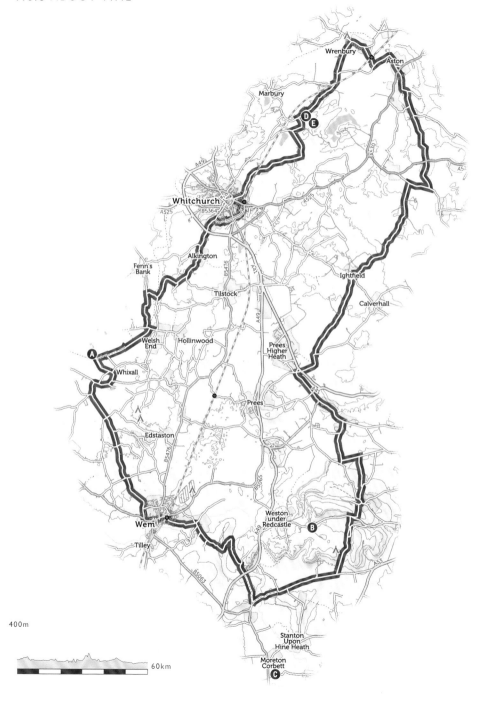

400m

60km

Combermere Monument

Moreton Corbet Castle

No. 9

SHROPSHIRE THRILLS

Big climbs and classic rough-stuff on the Long Mynd and the Stiperstones

———

Built on a sandstone crag encircled by a meander of the River Severn, Shrewsbury is the jewel of the Marches. With Wales less than ten miles away, the town grew rich on the Welsh cloth trade, and it was an important stopping point on the stagecoach road from London to Holyhead and onwards to Ireland. With typical Victorian boldness, not one but two railway lines come right into the town at a grandly turreted mock-Tudor castle directly below the town's actual castle. Architecturally, the town is a box of delights. The medieval street pattern of narrow passages, hidden corners, alleys and squares escaped both the bombs of the second world war and the town planners of the 1960s, and it now has a thriving ecosystem of independent shops, cafés, pubs, bars, boutique hotels and B&Bs. There's a surprise around every corner.

Sadly, the town is being slowly strangled by the ever-rising level of motor traffic and a hellish one-way system. The council has stalled on investing in good walking and cycling routes. As a result, the first and last miles of this route are a stark contrast to the very lost lanes of the rest of the ride. If you're coming by car, I suggest starting at Lyth Hill Country Park Ⓐ, where there is free parking, as this will spare you the sections through Shrewsbury's cycling-unfriendly outskirts. It will also shave a few miles from the ride, and you may

be glad of this, as the route climbs two of the highest and most iconic of Shropshire's hills, the Long Mynd and the Stiperstones.

From the town centre, a route through back streets leads to a series of shared-use footways beside busy A-roads. Once over the A5 and onto the road to Lyth Hill, the atmosphere becomes calmer and the views open up. Lyth Hill is a small ridge with big views across the Severn Vale to Wenlock Edge and the Stretton Hills. The narrow lanes with high-banked hedgerows that twist and turn through the fields are a reminder that Shropshire is perhaps the most rural of all English counties. The climbing begins in earnest on the Portway, an ancient route across Shropshire's open uplands that avoided the mud and mire of the densely wooded valleys. Stone axe-heads found along its course suggest that the Portway has been in use for at least five thousand years. From the 13th century onwards it was an important drovers' road to the livestock markets at Shrewsbury, especially after turnpike tolls were introduced on the main valley road (now the A49).

Above about 450m in elevation the Portway becomes a gravel track following the crest of the Long Mynd. The name of Shropshire's third highest hill derives from its Welsh name *Cefn Hirfynydd*, which means 'long mountain ridge'.

START & FINISH: Shrewsbury • DISTANCE: 44 miles / 71km • TOTAL ASCENT: 1085m
TERRAIN: Lanes, 4 miles on good gravel tracks, some urban roads
and a very short section of farm byway. Very challenging.

Shrewsbury

From the summit at Pole Bank there are views in all directions, with Cadair Idris in southern Snowdonia occasionally visible, 45 miles away to the west Ⓑ. It is especially glorious from mid-July to early September when flowering heather turns the moor purple. The Portway continues south along the ridge to Plowden, but my route descends from the gliding club at the top of Asterton Bank. This is one of the toughest road climbs in Britain, but there's no pain going down, only magnificent views. Just take care, as it is exceptionally steep.

Crossing the valley through Wentnor and Norbury is pure joy, on sunken wooded lanes. From Linley the climb of the Stiperstones begins, but it's steady going at first, through pine forests and eventually emerging onto the open moor. The hills are topped with rocky tors. These are not granite like on Dartmoor, but a very hard, quartzite sandstone that sparkles in the sun. Lead has been mined here since Roman times; The Bog was a major mining area from the 1730s to the 1880s and the volunteer-run visitor centre in the old, gas-lit schoolhouse tells the history of the place Ⓒ.

Along with the Long Mynd, the Stiperstones has long been a favourite with adventure-loving cyclists. There are some wonderful photographs from the 1930s of groups of local Shropshire club cyclists posing with their heavy steel bikes on the summit. My route keeps to the eastern flank, making use of a mostly rideable track Ⓓ via The Hollies farm and onto quiet lanes following the Habberley Brook to Pontesbury. On the way down, look out for the Gatten Valley Daffodil Field Ⓔ. In 2015, Jane Hulton-Harrop, a local farmer and supporter of the Marie Curie cancer charity, planted 170,000 daffodils to create a place for reflection and remembrance. They tend to come into bloom in early April.

In Pontesbury the peace of the last few hours riding is temporarily shattered, but there are more good, quiet lanes following National Cycle Route 44 via Shorthill to Annscroft. Here is the turning back to Lyth Hill, otherwise it's a straight shot back to Shrewsbury on Longden Road. Though part of the Sustrans National Cycle Network, and mostly downhill, it is not an especially pleasant road to ride, but unfortunately there's no better way back.

PUBS & PIT STOPS

RECTORY FARM, Woolstaston, Church Stretton, Shropshire. SY6 6NN (01694 751306) Traditional B&B in a beautiful half-timbered farmhouse dating from 1620.

BOTTLE AND GLASS INN, Picklescott SY6 6NR, United Kingdom (01694 751252) A bit early in the ride, but a characterful pub in a fine 17th-century building.

CROWN INN, Wentnor SY9 5EE (01588 650613) Family-run village pub serving locally-sourced food, hearty homemade pies and well-kept local ales. Small south-facing terrace. Rooms for overnight stays.

WENTNOR STORES, Rock Close SY9 5EP (01588 650113) Village stores for basic supplies in case the pubs are shut.

THE BRIDGES, near Ratlinghope SY5 0ST (01588 650260) A little off-route, but a great pub run by the Three Tuns Brewery at Bishop's Castle. Good food from local producers, including the pub's own kitchen garden.

BROW FARM CAMPSITE, near Ratlinghope SY5 0SR, United Kingdom (01588 650641) Rural camping among 12 acres of meadow on an ecologically-minded farm. Good value glamping pods also available. Close to The Bridges pub (above).

YHA BRIDGES, near Ratlinghope SY5 0SP (03452 602569) Since 1931 this has been a rural haven offering simple and affordable accommodation in an old Victorian school house. Close to The Bridges pub (above).

THE BOG VISITOR CENTRE, The Bog SY5 0NG (01743 792484) Lovely café in the lost mining village on the edge of the Stiperstones. Hot drinks and ice creams, homemade cakes and scones. March-October. Nearby is Nipstone Campsite (01743 792073) a tranquil car-free camping field with toilets and hot and cold running water.

Plenty of choice in Pontesbury though none of them especially good. There's a **CO-OP** on Hall Bank SY5 0RF for emergency supplies and the trad **CONNECTIONS CAFÉ** on Shrewsbury Road SY5 0QD (01734 790600).

BIKE SHOP: Trek, 53-54 Wyle Cop, Shrewsbury SY1 1XJ (01743 343775), Urban Bikes, The Market Hall, Claremont Street, Shrewsbury SY1 1QG (01743 365018), Dave Mellor Cycles, 9 New St, Frankwell, Shrewsbury SY3 8JN (01743 366662).

BIKE HIRE: Shrewsbury eBike Hire, 6 Claremont Hill, Shrewsbury SY1 1RD (01743 244800). This is a perfect ride to put an ebike through its paces on the hills.

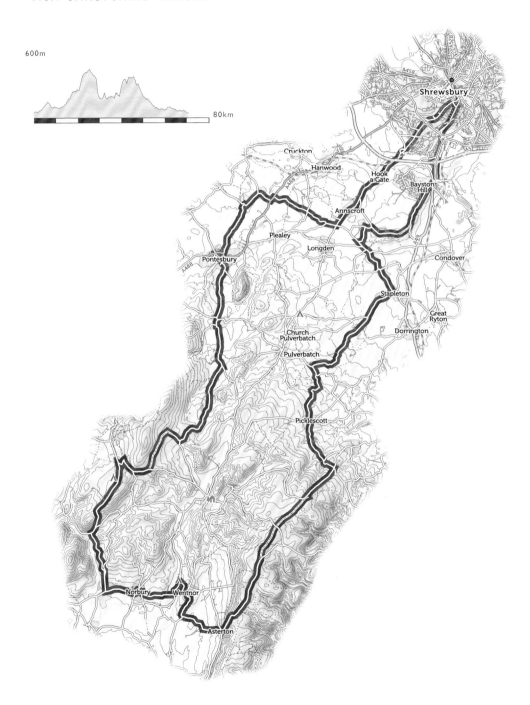

600m

80km

Shrewsbury

Cruckton
Hanwood
Hook
a Gate
Bayston
Hill
Annscroft
Plealey
Longden
Condover
Pontesbury
Stapleton
Great
Ryton
Church
Pulverbatch
Dorrington
Pulverbatch
Picklescott
Norbury
Wentnor
Asterton

A458
A488
A488
A49
A5

The Long Mynd

The Long Mynd

No. 10

OVER THE EDGE

From elegant Ludlow to Wenlock Edge
and the lofty heights of the Clee Hills

———

Ludlow is the perfect base for exploring southern Shropshire: head west into a labyrinth of lanes that lead to the Welsh border, or north, as in this route, into the broad valleys of Ape Dale and Corve Dale, the wooded slopes of Wenlock Edge and the two highest peaks in Shropshire. Expect deserted country lanes lined by hedgerows and some splendid trees, big views and just the right blend of climbing and easy pedalling.

The route out of Ludlow following National Cycle Route 44 is always a pleasure, passing beneath the walls of Ludlow Castle Ⓐ. Like all of England's early stone castles, it was built by Norman warlords to secure their newly conquered lands, an act of physical and psychological domination. The castle became the seat of the regional council which governed Wales and the Marches on behalf of the English crown right up to 1689, after which point the castle fell into disrepair. Following the River Teme upstream, the route crosses the river by the old mill at Bromfield and switches to the Teme's tributary, the River Onny. As there's no good cycling road along the valley towards Craven Arms it's best to cut the corner by climbing into Hope Dale and Ape Dale. Together with neighbouring Corve Dale, these are the most southerly 'dales' in England. South of here, such broad open valleys

such as these are commonly known as combes, denes and vales.

After crossing Ape Dale, the lane to Cardington has good views west to Caer Caradoc. Shropshire has many shapely hills and Caer Caradoc is one of the best. Cardington is a lovely village that oozes rustic charm and has a wealth of buildings from the 16th century and a few even older Ⓑ. Heading east, back across Ape Dale, the dark wooded scarp slope of Wenlock Edge looms ahead. The long limestone ridge is a defining landscape feature of the area. The lane ascends to a col between the two highest points on the ridge. Though steep in places it is not an especially long climb and, near the top, it's worth stopping at Wilderhope Manor Ⓒ. For centuries, this Grade I listed Elizabethan manor house represented the wealth and privilege of its various owners but by the 1930s it had fallen into disrepair. Seeing an opportunity, the Cadbury family of Birmingham chocolatiers stepped in. They bought and restored the house and donated it to the National Trust on condition that it be used as a youth hostel.

After a joyful descent into Corve Dale there are a few miles of flat riding before the road heads uphill once again, this time for the climb up Brown Clee Hill. On the way up, look out for a plain stone chapel in a field, on the

---

START & FINISH: Ludlow • DISTANCE: 49 miles / 79km • TOTAL ASCENT: 995m
TERRAIN: Lanes and some very short sections on A and B roads. Challenging.

Wilderhope Manor

Bromfield Mill

left of the lane a mile past Bouldon. Stepping inside is magical, like time travelling back to the 12th century Ⓓ.

At 540m, Brown Clee Hill is the highest point in Shropshire. The climb via the hamlet of Cockshutford is on a balcony lane that follows the contour of the hill at around 350m. The climb to the top is an optional extra in this ride, as it requires taking on a climb so severe that it that defeated Simon Warren, the racing cyclist and author of the *100 Greatest Cycling Climbs* books. Warren describes Abdon Burf Ⓔ as "an arrow straight line of 20-25% slope, no respite, no deviation just a direct line of pain, and it beat me. I put my foot down not once, not twice, but three times." For touring cyclists there is no shame in walking, and if you've got the time and energy, it's well worth it. The views from the top are unbeatable.

The route around Brown Clee Hill ends with a sublime traffic-free run on the estate road through Burwarton Park. Beyond Burwarton is Stoke St Milborough, a medieval pilgrimage place owing to a well dedicated to St Milburga, a 7th century Mercian princess Ⓕ. Though only very recently converted from paganism themselves, Anglo-Saxon elites used the spread of Christianity to consolidate their own political power. The cult of St Milburga flourished in medieval England; she is the subject of dozens of stories and legends.

The spring water at her well, which still flows freely today, was believed to heal sore eyes.

The B4364 is the direct route back to Ludlow, but the traffic can be fast so I opt for a more meandering route on farm lanes via Bitterley, which also offers a closer encounter with Titterstone Clee Hill. Though 7m lower than Brown Clee Hill, it has a more dramatic, mountain-like form. Amazingly, it is the only hill in Britain to be named on the Hereford *Mappa Mundi*, the largest surviving medieval map of the world. The map is now displayed in Hereford Cathedral, thirty miles to the south. Both of the Clee hills are capped by a layer of dark, volcanic Dhu Stone, one of the hardest rocks in the British Isles.

The church in Bitterley has a timber witcheshat spire built during a Victorian restoration. In the churchyard is a fairly rare sight: an intact medieval cross which has been standing here for around 700 years Ⓖ. A farm byway and the charmingly named Squirrel Lane lead back to Ludlow.

PUBS & PIT STOPS

LUDLOW FARMSHOP, Bromfield SY8 2JR (01584 856000) Large farm shop and kitchen-café. A good place to buy picnic supplies.

THE ROYAL OAK, Cardington SY6 7JZ (01694 771266) Characterful 15th-century pub with low-beamed rooms, quarry tiled floors and inglenook fireplace. Try the famous cider-infused 'fidget pie'.

NORTH HILL FARM B&B, near Cardington SY6 7LL (01694 771532) Good value B&B in an exceptional location above Cardington.

LEY HILL FARM, Cardington SY6 7LA (01694 771366) 4-acre camping field on this caravan and campsite, hot showers and basic facilities.

ALDERWOOD GLAMPING, Willstone SY6 7HW. Comfortable and well-equipped bell tents at the foot of Caer Caradoc.

YHA WILDERHOPE MANOR, Longville in the Dale TF13 6EG (03453 719149) Stay in a stunning Elizabethan manor house for youth hostel prices.

THE TALLY HO INN, Bouldon SY7 9DP (01584 841811) Small, welcoming rural pub. Food served but worth calling ahead to book.

THE PHEASANT, Neenton WV16 6RJ (01746 787955) Two miles off-route, but worth the detour to stay overnight at this superb community-owned pub that serves great food.

LUDLOW BREWING CO, Station Drive, Ludlow SY8 2PQ (01584 873291) Stylish brewery tap in a restored Victorian railway shed, lots of outside seating. Bar food.

BIKE SHOP: Epic Cycles, Coder Rd, Ludlow SY8 1XE (01584 705042).

BIKE HIRE: Wheely Wonderful, Petchfield Farm, Elton, near Ludlow SY8 2HJ (01568 770755).

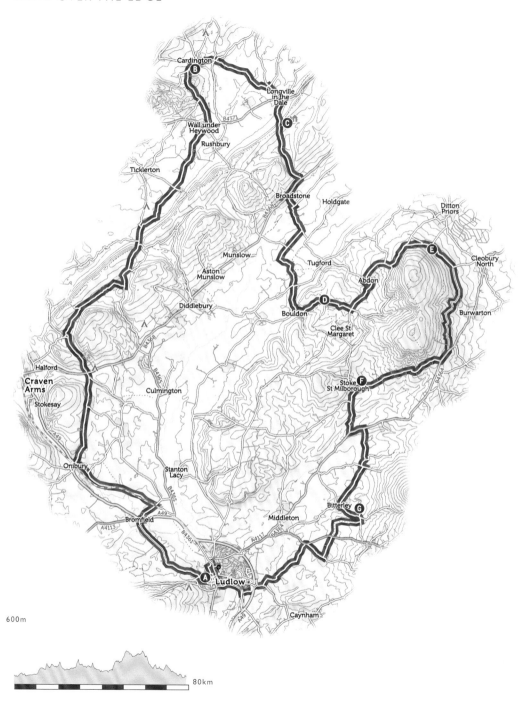

600m

80km

Brown Clee Hill

Titterstone Clee Hill

TAKE IT TO THE BRIDGE

A journey back in time through Shropshire's remarkable
geology to the crucible of the Industrial Revolution

———

No town on the River Severn — with the possible exception of Shrewsbury — has a more impressive setting than Bridgnorth. High Town clusters around a castle perched atop a bright red sandstone cliff and overlooks Low Town, down by the river's edge. Since the 1890s the two have been connected by a funicular railway. Bridgnorth is also the northern terminus of the Severn Valley heritage railway, whose steam and diesel trains ply the scenic 16-mile line from Kidderminster — bicycles carried free. This route is also accessible from the main line at Wellington, but starting in Bridgnorth gives a better sense of flow, with the hillier part of ride in the first half.

Leaving the town, the hills of this part of Shropshire are immediately apparent. They line up in a series of long ridges, like waves approaching the shore. Bridgnorth is built on a small outcrop of New Red Sandstone, the compressed and weather-sculpted remains of sand dunes that were formed nearly 300 million years ago, when Shropshire looked more like the Sahara. Just a few miles further on, and 100 million years further back in geological time, you're riding on Old Red Sandstone, formed when Shropshire was underwater.

Climbing Wenlock Edge you'll swap Old Red Sandstone for even older limestone. This long wooded ridge between Telford and Ludlow is the remains of a tropical ocean reef that once teemed with aquatic life Ⓐ. The fossil-rich hill was a fitting setting for the poet A. E. Housman's meditation on the transience of human cares and concerns, when compared with the timescales of nature and the land. Ralph Vaughan Williams set Housman's verse to music in his song cycle "On Wenlock Edge". In more recent times, the nature writer Paul Evans writes his long-running 'Country Diary' for the Guardian newspaper from here.

Soon after crossing Wenlock Edge and another smaller ridge that comes after it, there are a couple of buildings well worth a closer look. The Langley Chapel is a barn-like building adjacent to a farm where a much larger, and grander, moated hall once stood. The chapel is now in the care of English Heritage, on account of its early 17th century furniture and fittings, still largely intact Ⓑ. A mile on is Acton Burnell Castle, a fortified manor house built in the 1280s by Robert Burrell, a prominent Shropshire landowner and close friend and advisor to Edward I Ⓒ. The king was a regular visitor, especially during his military campaigns to conquer Wales. Edward held an early meeting of parliament here in 1283, said to be the first where commoners were represented as well as the nobility. The meeting took place in

---

START & FINISH: Bridgnorth • DISTANCE: 41 miles / 67km • TOTAL ASCENT: 992m
TERRAIN: Lanes and 6 miles of unsurfaced rail-trail. Moderate to Challenging.

River Severn and the Wrekin

the great barn, the remains of which stand in the grounds of Concord College, a private international school.

Turning north-east and crossing the River Severn at Cressage Bridge Ⓓ the route heads for The Wrekin Ⓔ. This is another Shropshire hill that makes geologists go weak at the knees. Its complex amalgam of rocks includes some of exceptional antiquity: the remains of lava flows from volcanoes that erupted 680 million years ago, when Shropshire was a chain of volcanic islands, like Japan or the Antilles, at the meeting of two tectonic plates. There is a rough, steep but just about rideable track to the summit, which commands astonishing views in all directions. Looking due east across the Midlands, the next highest land is the Ural Mountains.

The remainder of the ride takes in a much more recent episode of Shropshire's epic geological history. Towards the end of the last Ice Age, around 12,500 years ago, glacial meltwaters cut a deep gorge through the underlying rock. This process changed the course of the River Severn forever: previously, it had flowed north into the River Dee. In carving the gorge the flood exposed deposits of coal, iron ore, fireclay and limestone — exactly the raw materials needed to make iron.

What set Coalbrookdale apart from other iron-making areas of Britain and, indeed, the world, was Abraham Darby's idea to use coke, a derivative of coal, instead of charcoal in the blast furnace. This not only reduced the cost of producing iron but freed iron production from the limited availability of wood as a fuel. Coalbrookdale can rightly claim to be the crucible of the industrial revolution. Refinements of Darby's process led to the production of the first iron rails (until then rails had been made of wood or carved from stone).

The crowning glory of the valley remains the world's first cast iron bridge which opened here in 1779 Ⓕ. Cycling through the gorge you'll pass several of the ten different museums that tell the story, including whole museums devoted to chinaware, tiles, clay pipes and, of course, iron.

After crossing the Severn on the Iron Bridge, the route follows the river downstream, for the most part on a traffic-free cycling and walking path along the trackbed of the old railway line.

About half the way to Bridgnorth, the trail passes through the grounds of Apley Hall, a vast Gothic-revival castle on the other bank of the river Ⓖ. Set among the steeply wooded banks of the Severn, you could imagine yourself somewhere in the Upper Rhine Valley. This may explain why Hitler is said to have earmarked the house, and the town of Bridgnorth itself, for his personal headquarters in the event of a successful Nazi invasion of Britain.

PUBS & PIT STOPS

LOWER HILL FARM CAMPSITE, Much Wenlock SY5 6NX (07966 491319) Glamping with wood fired hot tubs.

HALFWAY HOUSE ON THE WREKIN, TF6 5AL. On the track up the Wrekin, a kiosk café and garden; weekends and school holidays only.

THE HUNTSMAN, Wellington Road, Little Wenlock TF6 5BE (01952 503300) Village pub with rooms.

GREEN WOOD CAFÉ, 6 Station Road, Coalbrookdale TF8 7EG. Coffee, veggie/vegan-friendly street food, and nano-pub, part of a woodland crafts centre.

Plenty of choice in Ironbridge including **GREYS OF SHROPSHIRE,** 26 High Street TF8 7AD (01952 432522), **ELEY'S PORK PIES,** 13 Tontine Hill TF8 7AL (01952 432504), **THE CORACLE MICROPUB,** 27 High Street TF8 7AD (01952 432664). **EIGHTY SIX'D,** 1A Waterloo Street TF8 7ED (01952 432620) is the pick of the cafés for coffee, lunches and more.

IRONGORGE CAMPING, Strethill Road, Coalbrookdale TF8 7EY (01952 433047) Camping and glamping on a 14-acre smallholding.

IRONBRIDGE COALPORT YHA, Coalport TF8 7HT (0345 371 9325) In a former china works, well located for visiting nearby museums and industrial heritage.

THE BOAT INN, Jackfield TF8 7LS (01952 884483) Old-school boozer with a big garden. Cash only.

WOODBRIDGE INN, Coalport TF8 7JF (01952 882054) Large, popular inn with a big garden on the riverbank.

COALPORT STATION HOLIDAYS, Station House, Coalport TF8 7JF (01952 885674) Stay in historic GWR rolling stock converted into comfortable holiday homes for 4 to 6 people.

RAILWAYMAN'S ARMS, 1 Hollybush Rd, Bridgnorth WV16 5DT (01746 760920) Real ale pub on the platform of the Severn Valley steam railway.

RIDLEYS ON THE RIVER, 15 Bridge Street, Lowtown, Bridgnorth WV16 4BE (01746 765333) Friendly riverside gastropub known for its pies and Sunday roasts.

BIKE SHOP: Clee Cycles, Station Works, Hollybush Road, Bridgnorth WV16 4AX (01746 763120)

Acton Burnell Castle

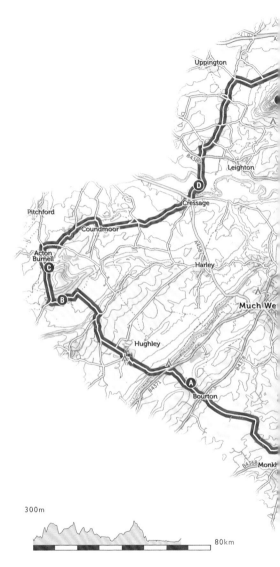

300m

80km

Bridgnorth

Apley Hall

No. 12

SEVERN UP

From historic Worcester to salty Droitwich, cheerful Stourport
and back through Worcestershire's famous fruit orchards

———

The city of Worcester grew at a place where the River Severn could be crossed by a ford. The first bridge was built in medieval times and was the only one in a 50-mile stretch of the river. Even today, the surprisingly limited number of bridges across the Severn shapes any exploration of this part of Worcestershire. My route heads upstream on the flatter farmland on the eastern side of the river, crossing at Stourport and returning via the more hilly terrain of the western side.

For more than a thousand years, Worcester has been a commercial, political and religious centre. The Romans enlarged existing Iron Age fortifications and the Anglo-Saxon kings of Mercia reused the Roman city walls as part of their defences against the Vikings who had conquered northern England. They also gave Worcester a bishop and a cathedral. Construction of the present cathedral began in 1084 and took more than 400 years. As a result, it contains every style of medieval English church architecture, from Norman to Perpendicular. It was in Worcester that Charles II suffered the final defeat that ended the Civil War. During the Second World War, it was to Worcester that Winston Churchill planned to relocate the British government in the event of a successful German land invasion. Coincidentally, it is just

28 miles from Adolf Hitler's planned HQ in Bridgnorth (see Ride No. 11).

The route out of Worcester follows National Cycle Route 46, initially on a lovely path between the river and the racecourse. On race days, when the riverside path is closed, there's an alternative path on the town side of the racecourse. The ride follows the course of the Severn, then switches to the canal that was built to carry salt from the brine pits at Droitwich. Beneath Worcestershire lie vast deposits of salt, the evaporated remains of an inland sea. For reasons not fully understood, the salty spring water that bubbles up to the surface at Droitwich is fully saturated with salt, making it ten times stronger than sea water and on a par with the Dead Sea. Boiling a litre of Droitwich brine can yield 260 grams of solid salt. The Romans, who paid their soldiers a regular allowance of salt (from where the word 'salary' is derived) named the town *Salinae*, while the Anglo-Saxons knew it as Saltwich. At the time of the Norman conquest, it's estimated the town was producing 1,000 tons of salt a year. Saltwich became Droitwich when King John granted the town its charter in 1215 ('droit' meaning 'right' or 'entitlement' in the French spoken by the English ruling class). 'Spa' was added when Droitwich attempted, not very successfully, to reinvent itself as a Victorian spa

---

START & FINISH: Worcester • DISTANCE: 42 miles / 67km • TOTAL ASCENT: 682m
TERRAIN: Lanes and three short unsurfaced sections of canal towpath, bridleway and byway. Moderate.

Worcester

Droitwich S?

town, boasting Britain's only brine baths. In Vines Park, there is a replica brine pit and an explanation of the salt-making process Ⓐ.

The canal provides a tranquil way through town. It's then lanes through some gently rolling farmland to Hartlebury Castle, an official residence of the bishops of Worcester from 855 to 2007. Both house and grounds, which houses the Worcester County Museum, are now open to visitors (£) Ⓑ. Soon after, the route picks up an old railway line for an easy, traffic-free entry to Stourport-on-Severn.

At the confluence of the rivers Severn and Stour (and the Stour's man-made twin, the Staffordshire and Worcestershire Canal), Stourport was a key node in the canal network of rapidly industrialising Georgian England. The town grew as goods moving into and out of the West Midlands passed through its locks, basins and wharfs. Much of the red brick Georgian architecture remains as an attractive backdrop to a town that, though miles inland, has a breezy, maritime feel and has long been popular with day-trippers.

Compared to the gently rolling farmland of the Worcestershire plain, the lands west of the Severn is hillier, more wooded and altogether more interesting, with a dense network of lanes and tracks perfect for exploring by bike. Having said that, the final ascent of Abberley Hill is a beast of a climb so it's worth taking your time. An essential stop in the village is the 12th century church of St Michael, which stands in atmospheric state of arrested ruin Ⓒ.

A climb this tough deserves more of a reward than simply shooting down the other side, and this is delivered in spades in the form of a wonderful byway through the grounds of Abberley Hall, past the deer park and beneath an ornate 50-metre-tall clock tower Ⓓ. A prominent local landmark, it's known as Little Ben due to its resemblance to London's iconic tower and bell – Big Ben.

After crossing the B4203 the ride takes a glorious balcony lane along the western flank of Woodbury Hill. Look out across the Teme Valley and the spires and farms of Worcestershire poet A. E. Housman's 'blue remembered hills'. At the end of the lane is a large flooded quarry rich in fossil-bearing mudstone Ⓔ.

The last part of the ride takes in two icons of Worcestershire: its fruit orchards and the composer Edward Elgar. The route follows quiet lanes past rows of trees that shimmer with white and pink blossom in late spring and groan with apples and pears come the autumn, then passes the house at Lower Broadheath where the great composer was born. The modest little red brick cottage is now cared for by the National Trust (£) Ⓕ; next door is the modern Elgar Centre which hosts regular concerts and other events. Elgar was a dedicated cyclist and his friend and riding companion Rosa Burley recalled how "as we rode, he would often become silent and I knew that some new melody or, more probably, some new piece of orchestral texture, had occurred to him". The final miles into Worcester are along the kind of unsurfaced lanes and byways that Elgar would have ridden on Mr Phoebus, his prized Royal Sunbeam, a heavy upright bicycle with eye-catching high-gloss enamel paintwork.

PUBS & PIT STOPS

THE PUMP HOUSE, Waterworks Road, Worcester WR1 3EZ (01905 734934) Community café in a grand Victorian waterworks.

THE MUG HOUSE, Claines WR3 7RN (01905 456649) Built in a churchyard, this 700-year-old beamed pub has a 1930s wood panelled interior including a traditional serving hatch.

CHURCHFIELDS FARM, Salwarpe WR9 0AF (01905 451289) Farm-to-fork café and ice cream parlour, and reviving the Droitwich tradition of salt making.

HAYLEY'S KITCHEN AT HARTLEBURY CASTLE, Hartlebury DY11 7XZ (01299 251901) Airy café in the grounds of the manor house - no admission fee required for café.

Plenty of choice in Stourport-on-Severn including **WINDLASS CAFÉ** (1 Severn Side DY13 9EN, 01299 871742), **BLOSSOMS TEA ROOM** (18 York Street DY13 9EE, 01299 829442), **GREENS VEGAN CAFÉ** (36 High Street DY13 8BA, 01299 827995) and **OLIVER'S COFFEE BOAT** (DY13 9EN), a canalboat in the lower canal basin.

MANOR ARMS, Abberley WR6 6BN (01299 890300) Upmarket dining pub with rooms.

CHIM DOO THAI, Bury End Farm, Wichenford WR6 6XY (07583 163191) Highly rated Thai restaurant on a farm, open for lunch and evening meals.

MASONS ARMS, Castle Hill, Wichenford WR6 6YA (01886 889064) Large food-oriented pub.

THE DEWDROP INN, Lower Broadheath WR2 6RR (01905 640012) Smart country pub with rooms. Food served all day.

THE PAUL PRY, 6 The Butts, Worcester WR1 3PA (01905 28992) Edwardian era pub with a lavish tiled interior.

KING CHARLES II, 29 New Street, Worcester WR1 2DP (01905 726100) Oak clad walls, roaring fires and a dungeon. Said to be King Charles II's escape route after losing the Civil War.

BIKE SHOP: Barbourne Bicycles, 45 Barbourne Road, Worcester WR1 1SA (01905 729535), Worcester Cycle Centre, Main Road, Hallow, Worcester WR2 6LD (01905 611123), Stourport Specialist Cycles, 106 The Birches, Stourport-on-Severn DY13 9NR (01299 826470).

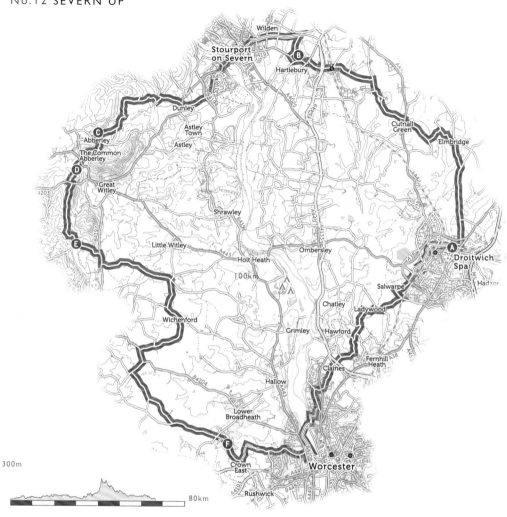

Wilden
Stourport on Severn
Hartlebury
B
Dunley
Astley Town
Astley
C Abberley
The Common Abberley
D
Great Witley
Shrawley
Little Witley
Holt Heath
E
100km
Wichenford
Ombersley
Chatley
Ladywood
Grimley
Hawford
Hallow
Claines
Fernhill Heath
Lower Broadheath
Cutnall Green
Elmbridge
A Droitwich Spa
Hadzor
Salwarpe
F Crown East
Worcester
Rushwick

300m
80km

Stourport-on-Severn

Abberley Hall

Woodbury Quarry

I HEAR A SYMPHONY

A circuit of the Malvern Hills in the tyre tracks of Edward Elgar

———

The Malvern Hills have made a greater contribution to science and culture than any other hills of their modest size and elevation. This may be because they appear bigger than they really are. Rising above the plains of Worcestershire, Gloucestershire and Herefordshire, they are visible for many miles as a distinctive chain of volcano-like peaks which rise "in a Pirramidy fashion on ye top", as the traveller Celia Fiennes noted in the 1690s. They are not old volcanoes, of course, though their rocks were formed deep within the earth's crust - igneous granites and diorites and granites, and metamorphic schists and gneiss - hundreds of millions of years before the sedimentary rocks that shape most of the English landscape. It's not just rockhounds who flock to the Malverns. They've been a muse to writers, from the 14th century poet William Langland who chose the hills as the setting for *Piers Plowman*, to Kazuo Ishiguro via Elizabeth Barrett Browning, C. S. Lewis, J. R. R. Tolkien and W. H. Auden. But perhaps it's the composer Edward Elgar who has become most closely associated with the hills and their surrounding landscape. He lived within sight of the Malverns for about 55 of his 76 years and explored the area both on foot and by bicycle, often composing music as he went. Ken Russell's 1962 drama-documentary *Elgar: Portrait of a*

Composer contains a brilliant recreation of such a ride; it can be found on YouTube.

This ride begins in Ledbury, a perfect base for exploring both the Malvern Hills and Herefordshire's cider country. You could also start in Malvern itself, but this would leave the (optional) ascent of Worcestershire Beacon until the very end of the ride. Starting at Ledbury means you can tackle it with fresher legs. From Ledbury the route heads straight uphill, onto the ominously named Cut Throat Lane. After crossing the railway line, the climb to the crest of the Malvern Hills begins at Colwall Green, along a wooded lane. At the junction with the B4232 is the Evendine spring, considered by connoisseurs to be among purest and best tasting of all of Malvern's celebrated springs Ⓐ. The purity of Malvern water is down to the hardness of the ancient rocks, and their fine cracks that filter out impurities. It takes six to eight weeks for rain to percolate through the rock and emerge at a spring. The water from Evendine's spout flows freely into a concrete trough, making it a good place to fill your water bottles for the day.

The road continues on a gentle climb along the wooded corniche of Jubilee Drive, one of Elgar's favourite rides. At the junction opposite possibly the most elegant bus shelter in England, you'll decide whether or not to head up Beacon Road

---

START & FINISH: Ledbury • DISTANCE: 37 miles / 60km • TOTAL ASCENT: 872m
TERRAIN: Lanes, quiet B-roads and an optional gravel climb up
to the Worcestershire Beacon. Moderate.

Leigh Court tithe barn

to the summit Ⓑ. The track is steep but perfectly rideable and the views are ample reward for the effort. Over the centuries much effort has been expended to determine just how far it is possible to see from the Worcestershire Beacon. Some claiming to have seen landmarks as far south as Exmoor and the Mendips, as far north as Cheshire and Stafford-shire, east to Leicestershire and Northamptonshire, and deep into Wales in the west. Computer analysis has confirmed that 19 historic counties of England and Wales are potentially visible, on a clear day.

From the pass at Wyche Cutting it's a steep descent into Malvern, so hold onto your brakes. With its famous spring water, clean air and attrac-tive surroundings, Malvern became one of the most successful spa towns in Victorian England.

By 1855 there were nearly a hundred hotels and guesthouses, hosting celebrity patients including Charles Darwin, Florence Nightingale and Alfred Tennyson. The coming of the railway opened the floodgates to day-trippers from the Black Country, Bristol and Manchester. As spa fever waned, many of the larger hotels were converted into private boarding schools. The town has more than its fair share of splendid buildings: the medieval priory and abbey gateway, the grand villas and hotels from the spa boom years, the exquisite painted metalwork of the railway station and the Edinburgh Dome, a 1970s pneumatically inflated concrete structure that's the sports hall of Malvern St James girls' school Ⓒ.

After picking a way through Malvern Link, it's

back onto lanes passing through farms and fields to Leigh Court, where a magnificent medieval tithe barn stands beside the River Teme. It is a masterpiece of carpentry, and Britain's largest cruck-framed structure (made from curved timbers) Ⓓ. From here the route exchanges the set-piece splendour of the Malvern Hills for a labyrinth of lost lanes, loosely following the Leigh Brook upstream to Alfrick, over the Suckley Hills and into the valley of the River Frome. This is a landscape of vineyards, hop fields, apple orchards and market gardens, on gently rolling hills. All evocative of a swirling Elgar composition. For the final crescendo, the route takes in Raycomb Lane, a glorious balcony lane on the western slope of the Oyster Hill Ⓔ. With a view across the Vale of Leadon, it will have you humming *Nimrod* as you coast into Ledbury.

PUBS & PIT STOPS

THE KETTLE SINGS TEAROOM, Jubilee Drive, Upper Colwall WR13 6DN (01684 540244) Café serving brunches, light lunches, cakes and ice cream.

Plenty of options in Great Malvern. Try **ST ANN'S CAFÉ** WR14 4RF (01684 560285) for the authentic Victorian spa experience (after climbing the 99 steps), or **MAC & JAC'S** 23 Abbey Road WR14 3ES (01684 573300) for good coffee and brunch classics.

ALFRICK & LULSLEY COMMUNITY SHOP, Alfrick WR6 5HJ (01886 832862) Outstanding community shop and café with seating inside and out.

THE MAJORS ARMS, Halmond's Frome WR6 5AX (01531 640261) Small country pub with stunning views from the terrace. B&B available.

THE MOATS B&B, Coddington HR8 1JW (01531 640039) Cosy, sensibly-priced rooms in a handsome, half-timbered house possibly dating back to Tudor times.

FARMER'S ARMS, Wellington Heath HR8 1LS (01531 634776) Sprawling country pub with plenty of outside tables and decent food.

Plenty of choice in Ledbury. **THE PRINCE OF WALES** Church Lane HR8 1DL (01531 577001) is a popular real ale pub down a little alleyway and there's good fish and chips nearby at **Y PASS,** 5 The Homend HR8 1BN (01531 632843).

BIKE SHOP: Cycles Clements, 6 Bank Crescent, Ledbury HR8 1AA (01531 632213); Detour, 41 Worcester Road, Malvern WR14 4RB (01684 891555).

BIKE HIRE: Ledbury Cycle Hire, Old Kennels Farm, Bromyard Road, Ledbury HR8 1LG (01531 635024).

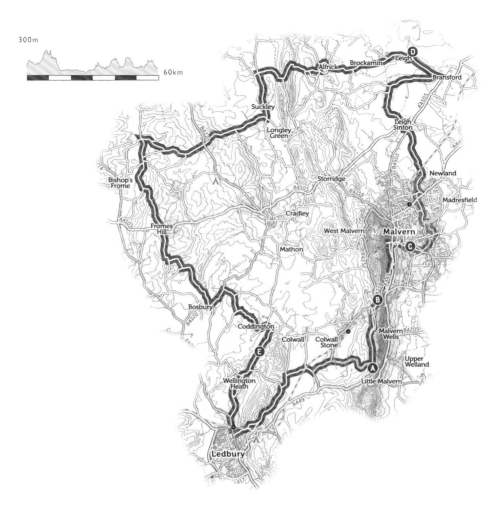

300m

60km

Edinburgh Dome, Great Malvern

Great Malvern

Malvern Hills

GLOUCESTERSHIRE

ROADS LESS TRAVELLED

A feast of ridgeways and holloways in a landscape of cider and poetry

———

The countryside between the River Leadon and the River Wye is little visited, yet among the most rewarding places to explore by bicycle. Set among wooded hills, it is a patchwork of small fields, orchards, vineyards and market gardens criss-crossed by a dense network of winding lanes. This is one of England's main cider-making areas; in late spring the orchards are bedecked in blossom, while in late autumn the boughs are laden and the cider mills hum as the harvest is pressed. Wedged between a sandstone ridge and the River Leadon, Ledbury is a small, handsome market town with a wealth of 'black and white' timber-framed Tudor and Elizabethan buildings and a wealth of small independent shops, pubs, restaurants and cafés. The town hosts the biggest annual poetry festival in the UK, a ten-day extravaganza of the spoken word that includes readings, workshops, exhibitions and even poetry bike rides.

From Ledbury the route heads west through the small village of Little Marcle and up Marcle Hill. This is one of several north-south ridges in the area, and there is a tremendous woodland bridleway along the crest, with views in both directions Ⓐ. It's exactly the kind of track that justifies a bike that's capable of a little riding off-road, but if you prefer to stick to the tarmac, this requires a short descent to Winslow Mill

and a climb back up to the ridge. The 164-metre high mast on Ridge Hill is the tallest structure in Herefordshire, beaming television and radio into homes across the region. There is a clear line of sight south to May Hill, a broad dome with a distinctive clump of trees on the top. After Ridge Hill comes another five-star ridgeway with views across the broad valley of the River Wye to the Black Mountains in Wales Ⓑ.

Briefly circling back towards Ledbury, the route passes Weston's Cider Mill, one of the UK's biggest producers Ⓒ. Just beyond is the village of Much Marcle, the hub of an annual Big Apple weekend that celebrates cider making, with events across nine local venues, from Gregg's Pit, where small batches of cider and perry are produced using artisanal methods, to Hellens, a beguilingly rambling and ramshackle manor house. The house is open to the public a few days each week in the summer; bookings are required to see the house, but the gardens and grounds are free to visit. Much Marcle church is well worth a visit at any time of year Ⓓ. Its treasures include the 14th century effigies of Walter de Helyon (cheery and colourful, in wood), Blanche Mortimer (exquisite and ethereal, in stone), some lavish Victorian stained-glass windows and six Green Men (an ancient symbol of rebirth, the Green Man has foliage sprouting from his mouth

---

START & FINISH: Ledbury • DISTANCE: 40 miles / 64km • TOTAL ASCENT: 866m
TERRAIN: Lanes and a 1½ mile section of mostly rideable
woodland bridleway. Moderate.

and sometimes ears and nostrils). Outside is an ancient yew tree with a bench inside its hollow core.

After crossing beneath the M50 motorway, another great ridge road runs from Linton to Aston Crewes. It's then a short but punchy climb up the northern flank of May Hill, the highest hill in Gloucestershire. From the small car park there is a track to the summit Ⓔ. Though steep in places, much of it is rideable. The summit is crowned by a grove of Corsican pines ringed by an Iron Age ditch. The view encompasses the River Severn, the Cotswolds, the Forest of Dean, the Wye Valley, the hills of Monmouthshire, the Black Mountains and the Malvern Hills. On the night of 30 April, the Wyedean Pagan and Wiccan Society gather here to celebrate the ancient fire festival of Beltane. They carry on through the night to May Day morning, when local Morris troupes dance to greet the rising sun.

It's downhill to Newent, a historic market town blessed with dozens of fine old buildings. Yet compared to Ledbury, the town feels dusty and downtrodden. The town's famous onion fair has recently been revived as a modern festival with live music, an onion show and onion-eating contests. From Newent, wooded holloways and hedgerow-lined farm lanes lead into a quiet corner of rural Gloucestershire that was, for a half dozen young poets who lived in and visited the countryside around Dymock in the looming shadow of the first world war, an enchanted land. They wrote about everyday things in the cadences of everyday speech, a deliberate break from the lofty and embellished style of Victorian poetry. The American poet Robert Frost's sojourn here was his springboard to literary greatness. Indeed, his famous poem "The Road Not Taken", was a gentle jibe at his close friend and fellow writer Edward Thomas, who was notoriously indecisive. Widely misunderstood as praising those who take 'the road less traveled by' the poem is actually about the pain of indecision and the stories we tell ourselves about the decisions we make. On their many 'talks-walking', by day and by night, across fields and through woods, Frost encouraged Thomas to turn his pen to poetry. The results were quietly dazzling. In the hamlet of Leddington the cottages where the two friends and their families stayed in 1914 are still there Ⓕ.

Another of the 'Dymock Poets' was the young and charismatic Rupert Brooke. His sonnet "The Soldier" captures the heady and romantic sense of nationalism that prevailed at the start of the war, and was swept away by the grim reality — and futility — of trench warfare. Brooke died of blood poisoning on a troop ship on his way to Gallipoli and Thomas was killed by a shell at the Battle of Arras, only weeks after arriving at the front. Frost later put Thomas's decision to enlist down to the sting of cowardice he had felt after a confrontation with a shotgun-wielding gamekeeper who had accused the pair of trespassing.

PUBS & PIT STOPS

THE SCRUMPY HOUSE, Westons Cider Mill, The Bounds, Much Marcle HR8 2NQ (01531 660233) Café-restaurant serving good food from breakfast onwards, and cider.

THE ALMA INN, Linton HR9 7RY (01989 720355) The best pub in the area, well-kept real ales and simple but perfectly executed pub food.

OAK MEADOW CAMPING, Lilly Hall, Gorsley HR9 7SG (07715 407665) Rustic campsite with just 5 pitches.

PENNY FARTHING INN, Aston Crews HR9 7LW (01989 750366) Large, rambling country pub, good views from the garden. Food served.

INTERNATIONAL CENTRE OF BIRDS OF PREY, Boulsdon House, near Newent GL18 1JJ (01531 820286) Small café is open for drinks and light bites.

Plenty of choice in Ledbury. **THE PRINCE OF WALES** Church Lane HR8 1DL (01531 577001) is a popular real ale pub down a little alleyway and there's good fish and chips nearby at **Y PASS,** 5 The Homend HR8 1BN (01531 632843).

BIKE SHOP: Cycles Clements, 6 Bank Crescent, Ledbury HR8 1AA (01531 632213); Detour, 41 Worcester Road, Great Malvern WR14 4RB (01684 891555).

BIKE HIRE: Ledbury Cycle Hire, Old Kennels Farm, Bromyard Road, Ledbury HR8 1LG (01531 635024).

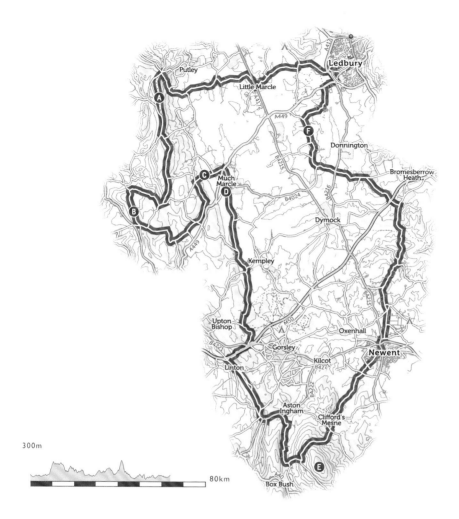

300m

80km

Much Marcle church

Much Marcle churchyard

No.15

FREEDOM OF THE FOREST

A gravel adventure in the Forest of Dean and Wye Valley

———

Like Romney Marsh on the south coast and the Isle of Axholme in Lincolnshire, the Forest of Dean is a place apart. An inland peninsula between the rivers Severn and Wye, it has a strong local identity and its own traditions and dialect. Though culturally English, its geology feels distinctly Welsh: an outcrop of the same coal and iron-rich limestone as the South Wales Valleys. Unlike the Valleys, though, the Forest has retained much of its woodland cover. With its deep dark woods and countless hollows, dingles, cliffs and caverns, it's just the landscape you'd expect to be inhabited by witches, fairies and trolls.

Roads through the heart of the Forest are straight and the drivers often go too fast, so this route combines quieter lanes with some of a vast network of traffic-free forest paths. Some of these are on the trackbeds of a railway that once connected the former industrial towns of Lydney, Coleford and Cinderford. The only part of the railway still running is the 4-mile-long steam heritage line between Lydney and Parkend. There are plans afoot for a new bike path along the same route.

From Parkend it's a pleasant warm up on the waymarked Family Cycle Trail heading north towards Cannop Ponds Ⓐ. With deposits of coal, iron and other minerals the Forest has an indus-

trial history stretching back many centuries, and the railway was built to service the mines and ironworks. A half mile to the west of the point where the trail crosses the B4266 is Hopewell Colliery, a museum and working mine that offers underground tours (£, booking essential) Ⓑ. As so often, people in Forest do things differently, and the custom of freemining is a case in point. This ancient law, which still stands today, gives the right to anyone born in the Forest who has worked underground for a year and a day, to stake a claim of their own. There are thought to be around 150 freeminers living today, though the recent closure of the Forest's last maternity unit has thrown into question whether the tradition can continue.

Following the Family Cycle Trail as far as the remains of Drybrook Road Station, it's then a sharp left onto more forestry tracks to the small village of Brierley. From here the road heads uphill to Ruardean. Set high on a ridge above the River Wye, Ruardean's church spire is a landmark for miles around - a stone rocket about to blast off into orbit. Above the south door is a rare 12th century carving of St George slaying the dragon. Ruardean's greatest gift to the world, however, could well be a good night's sleep. It was here that the Horlick family experimented with mixing fresh milk with extract of malted wheat

---

START & FINISH: Parkend • DISTANCE: 38 miles / 61km • TOTAL ASCENT: 895m
TERRAIN: Lanes and 12 miles of unsurfaced forest tracks. Challenging.

River Wye from Yat Rock

and barley, then reducing the resulting liquid into dried granules. At first they named it *Horlick's Infant and Invalids Food*. But the drink achieved worldwide success as plain old Horlicks. The granary building where it all started still stands, justa few doors from the village pub that is named, appropriately enough, the Malt Shovel Inn.

From Ruardean it's downhill all the way to the River Wye at Kerne Bridge. For the next 15 miles the route follows the Wye downstream, initially cutting across the river's extravagant meanders and passing close to Goodrich Castle, one of the Norman strongholds built to secure the border with Wales (English Heritage, £) ©. On the way into Symonds Yat, if you've got the legs for it, you can take a detour on the steep lane to Yat Rock, where the panorama of the Wye gorge is rightly celebrated as among the best views in Britain ⒟.

From Symonds Yat the Peregrine Trail continues where the tarmac road ends, on a riverside cycling and walking path along the track bed of the old Wye Valley Railway. It's a pleasant ride, crossing into Wales at the country's most easterly point in the Lady Park Wood nature reserve ⒠. The woodland has been left to develop without human interference since 1944 and is notable as an early instance of natural regeneration or 'rewilding'.

The Peregrine Trail ends at Wyesham, a village that's now effectively a suburb of Monmouth, on the other side of the Wye. The old railway line continues from Wyesham to Redbrook, and this is a good way to avoid the traffic on the A466. Though used by many locals, it's not an official cycleway, yet ⒡. Another route from Wyesham to Redbrook is the scenic route up Wyesham

Lane and onto Duffield's Lane. It's a cracking bit of rough stuff: mostly rideable but it can be soft under wheel after heavy rain ⓖ.

At Redbrook the old railway bridge across the river, now a footbridge, continues onto a forest track with a decent gravel surface. Crossing back into England on Bigsweir Bridge, whose elegant Georgian arches were cast in the foundries of Merthyr Tydfil, it's then a climb up to St Briavels. One of the prettiest villages in the Forest, it grew up around another Norman castle. Used variously as a courthouse, a royal hunting lodge, a weapons arsenal during Edward I's conquest of Wales, and as a debtors' prison, the castle now houses a youth hostel in its imposing gatehouse; the rest of the site is open to visitors (English Heritage, £).

From St Briavels, more lanes via Bream lead to the ruins of the Darkhill ironworks ⓗ. It was here that Robert Mushet perfected Henry Bessemer's process for producing high quality steel, though it was Bessemer, not Mushet, who reaped all the fame and fortune. The last miles back to Parkend are on another old railway line, a downhill run through some of the most beautiful woodland anywhere in the Forest.

PUBS & PIT STOPS

CANNOP PONDS KIOSK, GL15 4JS Outdoor café serving hot drinks, snacks and ice creams, right by the Family Trail.

THE MALT SHOVEL INN, Ruardean, Mitcheldean GL17 9TW (01594 543028) Stone-built village pub with simple, good value rooms for B&B.

INN ON THE WYE, Kerne Bridge HR9 5QS (01600 890872) Sprawling riverside pub with rooms, food served all day.

THE SARACEN'S HEAD INN, Symonds Yat East HR9 6JL (01600 890435) Hard to beat as a place to relax and watch the river flow by. Rooms for overnight stays.

BIBLINS YOUTH CAMPSITE, HR9 6DX (01600 890850) Large, idyllic riverside campsite, across the rope bridge. Managed by the Woodcraft Folk for school and youth groups but also open to family groups.

THE BOAT INN, Lower Penallt NP25 4AJ (01600 712615) Dating from 1650, a gorgeous country pub overlooking the river. Simple lunches served.

YHA ST BRIAVELS CASTLE, GL15 6RG (0345 3719042) Stay in an 800-year-old castle; budget dorm beds and private rooms available.

THE GEORGE INN, High St, St Briavels GL15 6TA (01594 530228) Attractive village pub serving Wadworth beers and food that's a cut above the usual.

THE PANTRY, High Street, St Briavels GL15 6TA (01594 530740) Volunteer-run community shop with a great range of cheese and other local produce.

BIKE SHOPS AND HIRE: Dean Forest Cycles, New Road, Parkend GL15 4HG (01594 368009), Pedalabikeaway, Cannop Cycle Centre, New Road, near Coleford GL16 7EH (01594 729000). Both combine bike shop, cycle hire and café.

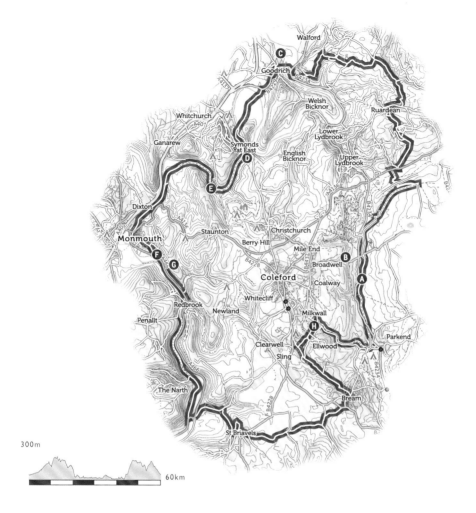

300m

60km

River Wye

St Briavels Castle

Bigsweir Bridge

AT THE CROSSROADS

A treasure trove of ancient ways in and around the capital of the Cotswolds

———

The arrival of the Roman Empire divided the Celtic tribes that ruled Britain during the Iron Age. Some resisted the powerful and sophisticated new arrivals. Others made amicable accommodations without any bloodshed, perhaps hoping that Roman rule might bring improvements to everyday life and some protection from rival tribes. The Dobunni tribe, which occupied the Cotswolds and the lower Severn Valley, sought peace. This may explain how their capital, at modern day Cirencester, became one of the main settlements in Roman Britain, known as *Corinium*. It stood at the meeting point of several Roman long-distance routes, the Fosse Way, the Ermin Way and Akeman Street. Then, as now, the town seems to have been well-to-do, with fine stone houses and evidence of a thriving craft-based economy including mosaic makers, glass makers, blacksmiths and goldsmiths.

Cirencester's railway line closed in 1964 and the nearest railhead is at Kemble; that's where this ride begins. On the way into Cirencester, tucked away among the suburban streets and new-build estates, are the remains of the Roman amphitheatre, big enough to seat 8,000 spectators Ⓐ. The site is free to enter. In the centre of town, the Corinium Museum tells Cirencester's history and contains thousands of artefacts including remains from the Roman era. The church on the Market Place is

quite something. Its three-storey south porch is the largest and most elaborate in England. Built of Cotswold stone, it was paid for by the fleeces of Cotswold sheep. Inside the church, beneath the intricately carved fan vaulted ceilings, are the ornate tombs of wealthy wool merchants, each one trying to outdo the other.

Like so many English towns, modern Cirencester is grappling with its traffic problems. Its one-way system and pedestrianised areas require a bit of careful negotiation, but from the Market Place the White Way leads straight out of town to the north. This is very likely a Roman road built to connect Corinium with a number of outlying villa settlements. Just after crossing the A417 dual carriageway, the White Way meets the Welsh Way. From the 1300s to the 1800s this was a route taken by Welsh drovers on the long journey taking cattle and other animals from hill farms in deepest Wales to the big livestock markets of south-east England. Today it's deserted — a truly gorgeous lost lane. Droving is a way of life that feels so very distant from our age, yet it is well recorded both in the written record, and in the form of clues in the landscape itself. The village of Barnsley must have been an overnight stopping point. It once had five inns and the ten-acre field by the church is where drovers paid a small fee so

---

START & FINISH: Kemble • DISTANCE: 48 miles / 77km • TOTAL ASCENT: 872m
TERRAIN: Lanes and a couple of very short sections on A-roads. Moderate.

their animals might rest and graze. Centuries of manure keeps the soil fertile to this day.

Beyond Barnsley, the Welsh Way meets Akeman Street, the Roman road heading due east towards St Albans. This crossroads — known as Ready Token — is a meeting of six roads and nine parish boundaries Ⓑ. The name has puzzled etymologists. It might derive from the Welsh *rhydd* and the Old English *tacen* meaning 'the way to the ford'. Others have suggested that the inn that once stood here insisted on payment in cash (i.e. ready tokens).

Akeman Street leads to a bridge over the River Coln. Here the route switches very briefly to the Salt Way, one of a number of routes that run north–south across the Cotswolds. Trains of packhorses would carry salt from the brine springs

at Droitwich (see Ride No. 12). At Lechlade, its southern end, the salt was loaded onto river barges for onward travel down the Thames. The Salt Way keeps to the higher ground, but the lane up the River Coln is more interesting, passing through a string of pretty Cotswold villages. For many, Bibury is the prettiest of them all. Arlington Row, the medieval wool stores built in the 1380s and later converted into weavers' cottages must be one of the most photographed streets in England. As well as appearing on countless Instagram posts, Arlington Row is on the inside cover of every British passport issued between 2010 and 2015 Ⓒ.

Further up the valley, after crossing the Fosse Way (now the fast A429), are the remains of Chedworth Roman Villa (£) Ⓓ. It is one of the largest so far discovered in Britain. From relatively spartan beginnings, about seventy years after the Romans arrived on British shores, the homestead grew in opulence, arranged around three sides of a courtyard. By the 4th century it included a wing with underfloor-heating, a dining-room with a fine mosaic floor, two separate sauna-steam complexes and a shrine to the water-nymphs thought to inhabit the spring which supplied fresh water to the villa. Coins recovered on the site show it was lived in well after the Roman Empire crumbled, suggesting some continuity of a sophisticated Romano-British culture into what are misleadingly dubbed the Dark Ages. Another twenty-two

Roman villas have been found within a ten-mile radius of Chedworth.

At the head of the valley there is no choice but uphill. Going west means cutting across the grain of the landscape, so there are a couple of climbs before crossing beneath Ermin Way, now the busy A417. From Winstone, the broad ridgeway named Jackbarrow Road makes for a good finishing straight. To the left of the road is the enormous Cirencester Park estate owned by the Earl of Bathurst and extending all the way into Cirencester Ⓔ. Some superb wooded lanes through Tarlton lead back to Kemble.

PUBS & PIT STOPS

Plenty of choice in Cirencester, but **LYNWOOD** opposite the church at 20 Market Place GL7 2NW (01285 420444), **KNEAD**, 12 Black Jack Street GL7 2AA (01285 653670) and **JACKS**, 44 Black Jack St GL7 2AA (01285 640888) are all excellent for coffee and cake, or picnic vittles.

THE T-BARN, Church Farm, Barnsley GL7 5EF UK (07717 756935) Luxurious shepherds' huts with wood-fired hot tubs, and a separate field with three bell tents and a handful of grass pitches for campers; campfires encouraged.

THE VILLAGE PUB, Barnsley GL7 5EF (01285 740421) Smart Cotswolds dining pub with rooms.

THE TWIG, Bibury GL7 5NL. Good coffee and more, an offshoot of the successful The Stump pizza and craft ale pub at Foss Cross.

BIBURY TROUT FARM CAF, Bibury GL7 5NL (01285 740215). Hot drinks, cakes and snacks from a hut beside one of Britain's oldest trout farms.

THE INN AT FOSSEBRIDGE, GL54 3JS (01285 720721) 300-year-old coaching inn with four acres of grounds running down to the river. Rooms available. Food served all day.

THE MILL INN, Withington GL54 4BE (01242 890204) Sprawling country pub with a garden by the river, pub grub.

THE COLESBOURNE INN, GL53 9NP (01242 870376) Handsome Wadworth brewery inn by a fairly busy road, rooms available. Food served all day.

THE BELL, Sapperton GL7 6LE (01285 760298) Stylishly rustic pub with a pleasant terrace and garden. Very good food. Rooms.

BIKE SHOP: Independent Bikeworks, 1 Templar Mews, Black Jack St, Cirencester GL7 2AA (01285 238184).

BIKE HIRE: Far Peak Hire Cycles, 1B The Hayloft, Far Peak, Northleach GL54 3AP (01285 700 370).

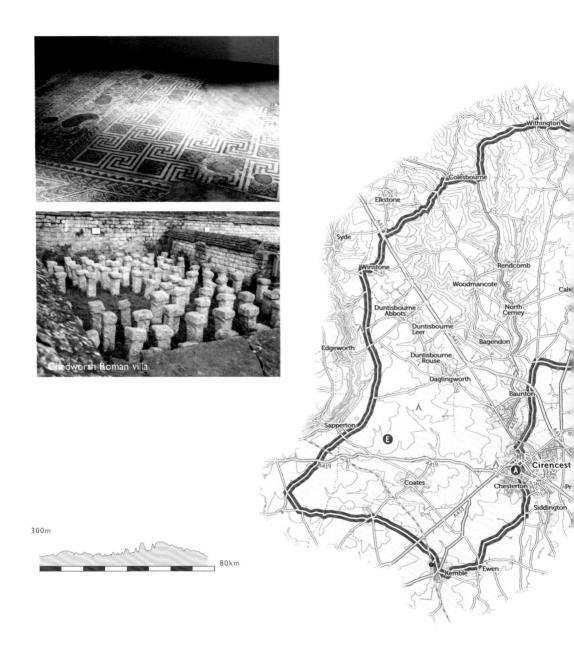

Chedworth Roman villa

300m

80km

Cirencester

The Bell at Sapperton

THIS CHARMING LAND

Through the honey-stoned heart of the Cotswolds
to its wild, windswept edge

———

With its rolling countryside, irresistibly charming towns and villages, and a dense network of roads, lanes and byways, the Cotswolds seem tailor-made for the pleasure-seeking cyclist. Yet the ever-rising tide of well-heeled second-homers driving about in outsized Range Rovers, added to the usual ebb and flow of day-trippers, means great care must be taken when stitching together a route, lest you end up on roads too busy for comfort. Dipping in and out of some of the most visited places in the heart of the Cotswolds, this route shows that, thanks to the bicycle, it is possible to have it both ways - experience the teeming honeypots and savour timeless moments of peace and solitude.

All roads (and rails) in this part of the Cotswolds lead to Moreton-in-Marsh, a lowland market town, which makes it a good starting point, though aesthetically it lacks the charm of its neighbouring towns and villages. After a short warm up along the course of the River Evenlode comes the first climb of the ride, up through Broadwell to Stow-on-the-Wold. True to its name, Stow sits atop a hill. That a town this size could have grown up here is thanks, in large part, to the presence of a reliable source of spring water. For centuries the main source of the town's drinking water, Stow Well is still flowing; you'll pass it as you enter the town Ⓐ. Visitors flock to St Edward's church to see the photogenic north door, framed by two veteran yew trees.

Leaving the crowds behind, a lane and a farm track head up Maugersbury Hill, along a ridge road then down through Little Rissington into Bourton-on-the-Water. Again, Cotswolds town names don't lie and the River Windrush, a tributary of the Thames, flows beguilingly through Bourton, and helps make the town one of the most heavily visited in the Cotswolds.

At Farmingham, the attractive stone shelter on the village green is a perfect spot for a break from the pedals. Fans of church architecture may want to make the short detour via Northleach (one of several churches that vie for the title of 'Cathedral of the Cotswolds') and Hampnett (colourful and once-controversial Victorian stencils). My route keeps to the north of the A40, heading straight for Turkdean on some of the best lanes anywhere in the Cotswolds. It's a steady climb across big arable fields dotted with shade-giving, wind-breaking stands of beech trees. The sense is of entering into a wilder and less populated Cotswolds. Take your time as you climb: the villages of Turkdean, Notgrove and especially Guiting Power are all worth a stop for a look around.

In medieval times the high-quality wool from large, fleecy Cotswold Lion sheep was prized by

---

START & FINISH: Moreton-in-Marsh • DISTANCE: 46 miles / 74km • TOTAL ASCENT: 929m
TERRAIN: Lanes and 3 miles of good gravel tracks. Challenging.

Broadway Tower

cloth merchants from Flanders to Venice. As land-owners sought to increase the size of their flocks they enclosed common grazing land, converted arable land to pasture and turfed out most of the peasantry. The abolition of the monasteries brought more land onto the market, and it was quickly snapped up by the ambitious and sharp-elbowed Tudor gentry. As sheep replaced sheaf, the population of the Cotswolds fell into decline while the wealth of landowners piled up. Those riches are still on display in the form of grand manor houses and fine parish churches. The miser of the displaced and dispossesed can only be imagined.

Beyond Guiting Power, the lane gives way to a magical gravel byway through Guiting Wood Ⓑ, then past Taddington, the source of the River Windrush, and onto the steep-edged crest of the Cotswold escarpment. This elevated lookout and a long-distance ridgeway is dotted with ancient landmarks, from burial mounds to hill forts. It's well worth sacrificing a little of that hard-earned altitude to see the village of Snowshill. Now cared for by the National Trust (£), the Tudor manor

house was once the home of the architect, artist, collector and archetypal English eccentric Charles Paget Wade Ⓒ. With a fortune derived from his family's sugar plantations of the Caribbean, Wade bought Snowshill Manor in 1919 after returning from military service on the Western Front. He began collecting at the age of 7 and eventually amassed more than 22,000 items — costumes, paintings, furniture, musical instruments, tools, toys, clocks, bicycles, weapons, armour and more. Wade had a tremendous eye for design, colour and craftsmanship. He arranged his collection in theatrical style in the big house, while he lived in a small cottage in his Arts-and-Crafts style garden. It's well worth stopping for a look around.

A couple of miles on from Snowshill is Broadway Tower, the second highest point in the Cotswolds and another monument to English eccentricity Ⓓ. The folly, modelled on a Saxon tower, was built for the Earl of Coventry, who could look up to it from the landscaped grounds of his country estate at Croome Park, fifteen miles away. Later, it was used by William Morris and his circle of pre-Raphaelite artists as a scenic bolt hole. It is said Morris started his campaign for the preservation of historic buildings while holidaying in the tower.

There must be something about the air on this ridge that attracts eccentricity as it was here, in the early 1600s, that a local lawyer Robert Dover had the bright idea to stage a Cotswold edition of the Ancient Greek Olympic Games. Staged in a natural amphitheatre on what's now known as Dover's Hill Ⓔ, the *Cotswold Olimpicks* included horse-racing, coursing with hounds, running, jumping, dancing, sledgehammer throwing, fighting with swords and cudgels, wrestling and, bizarrely, shin-kicking. It was wildly successful and drew crowds from all levels of society. The Puritans briefly closed it down but it continued into the 19th century as an increasingly raucous and drunken country fair. What finally put paid to the event was the privatisation of the common land on which it was held. It was revived for the Festival of Britain 1951 and again from 2016 onwards, with shin-kicking among the biggest draws. From Dover's Hill it's downhill to Chipping Campden, another handsome Cotswold market town and the last few rolling miles back to Moreton-in-Marsh.

PUBS & PIT STOPS

Plenty of choice in Stow-on-the-Wold, with: **STOW TOWN COFFEE** Sheep Street GL54 1AA (01451 832519), and **COACH HOUSE COFFEE**, Market Square GL54 1BQ (01451 831361) the pick of the bunch for coffee.

COTSWOLD CARP FARM CAMPING, Rissington Road, Bourton-on-the-Water GL54 2FH (01451 821795) Away from the crowds with just ten lakeside pitches.

THE NUTTERY, Notgrove GL54 3BS (07580 024457) Coffees, breakfasts, lunches, homemade cakes at this hip village hub.

Good choices at Guiting Power GL54 5TZ including the **OLD POST OFFICE** (01451 850701) village shop and café, the **FARMERS ARMS** (01451 850358), a classic Cotswold village pub with skittle alley, and the effortlessly stylish **HOLLOW BOTTOM** 01451 611111) for modern bistro fare.

THE PLOUGH INN, Ford GL54 5RU (01386 584215) Village pub with large garden, upmarket pub classics.

HAYLES FRUIT FARM, Winchcombe GL54 5PB (01242 602123) Quiet campsite, farm shop and tearoom on a family-run fruit farm, just off-route.

SNOWSHILL ARMS, WR12 7JU (01386 852653) 15th Century village inn in pretty Snowshill. Reasonably priced pub grub.

MORRIS & BROWNIE CAFÉ, Broadway Tower WR12 7LB (01386 852945) Coffee, cakes, lunches and cream teas with lots of outdoors seating.

THE BAKERS ARMS, Broad Campden GL55 6UR (01386 840515) Cosy drinkers' pub.

BIKE SHOP: Cotswold Cycles, 3 Cotswold Link, Moreton-in-Marsh GL56 0JU (01608 650933).

BIKE HIRE: Hartwells Cotswold Cycle Hire, High Street, Bourton-on-the-Water GL54 2AJ (01451 820405)

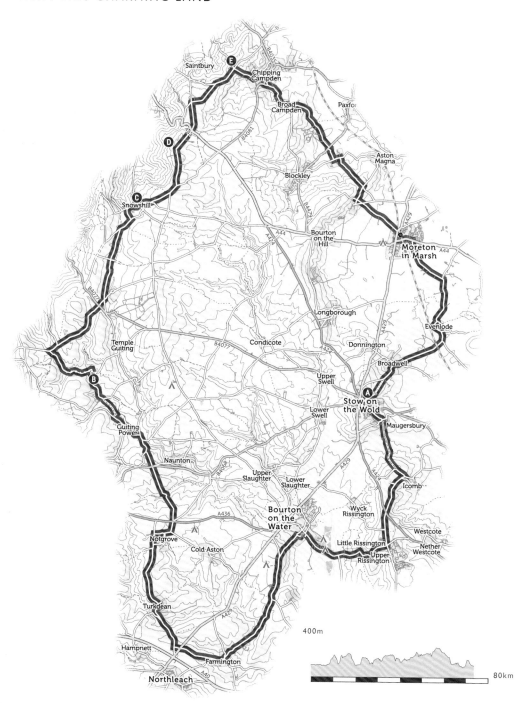

Saintbury

E Chipping
Campden

Broad
Campden

Paxfo

Aston
Magna

Blockley

D

B4081

Snowshill C

Bourton
on the
Hill

Moreton
in Marsh

A44

B4077

Temple
Guiting

Longborough

Condicote

Donnington

Evenlode

A424

A429

Broadwell

B

Upper
Swell

A Stow on
the Wold

Guiting
Power

Lower
Swell

Maugersbury

Naunton

B4068

Upper
Slaughter

Lower
Slaughter

A429

A424

Icomb

A436

Bourton
on the
Water

Wyck
Rissington

Westcote

Notgrove

Cold Aston

Little Rissington

Nether
Westcote

Upper
Rissington

400m

Turkdean

A429

Hampnett

Farmington

A40

Northleach

80km

Guiting Power

Stow-on-the-Wold church

HEART OF
ENGLAND

No.18

CANAL CITY

An urban exploration of Birmingham's waterways and urban greenways

---

As any proud Brummie will tell you, Birmingham has more miles of canal than Venice. Of course the UK's second biggest city is a bit more spread out, and doesn't quite match the Queen of the Adriatic for visual impact. But canals are intrinsic to Birmingham's history and are not without their moments of splendour. Half close your eyes as you're cycling through Gas Street Basin on a misty morning or darkening twilight and you might be transported to the iconic scenes of Birmingham's industrial heyday that were such a compelling element of the successful Peaky Blinders television drama. What's more, they provide a superb traffic-free cycle network connecting the city centre with the surrounding countryside.

This ride starts at Cambrian Wharf and heads north-east on the Birmingham & Fazeley Canal. Birmingham isn't a flat city, and you get a sense of the engineering challenges involved in building a network of waterways as you descend a series of locks that take the canal down a hill. As tall buildings rise on each side of the canal, bridges soar overhead, bearing roads and railways over the canal. The sensation is of descending into a kind of watery underworld. Always remember that the narrow canal towpath is shared with pedestrians and be prepared for some very steep and uneven paved surfaces. Ride carefully as you take it all in.

At the time of the Norman conquest, Birmingham was a small village, if that. The Domesday book records "five villagers and four smallholders with two ploughs". It got going as a medieval market town thanks to Warwickshire's growing livestock and wool trade. Birmingham was a stop on drovers' routes from Wales to the south-east of England. By the Tudor era Birmingham was still a relatively small but well-established town of blacksmiths and metal workers, making nails, knives, scythes, drills and other cutting tools as well as jewellery. Rapid growth meant that, by 1775, Birmingham was the third largest town in England after the port cities of London and Bristol, and growing faster than either.

Its success was down to proximity to raw materials in Staffordshire and the town's radical and free-thinking political tradition, a marked contrast to the hidebound feudalism of the landed aristocracy. Birmingham was a place where self-made merchants and manufacturers could prosper, and they did. The city was soon in the forefront of worldwide developments in science, technology, medicine, philosophy and natural history, moving from the scientific revolution into the industrial revolution. By 1791 Birmingham was being hailed as 'the first manufacturing town in the world'. As heavy industry took off elsewhere

---

START & FINISH: Birmingham • DISTANCE: 25 miles / 40km • TOTAL ASCENT: 349m
TERRAIN: Canal towpath, traffic free cycleways and quiet roads. Easy.

Spaghetti Junction

in the Midlands and the North, Birmingham came to specialise in intricate and high value products such as guns, locks, jewellery and watches. Fierce competition spurred innovation in techniques and materials in 'the city of a thousand trades'.

Heading north, the canal passes through the industrial estates of Aston, once home to Hercules, the biggest of Birmingham's many bicycle companies in the early 20th century. By the end of the 1930s it was the biggest bike manufacturer in the world. The canal then arrives beneath the concrete pillars and steel girders of the Gravelly Hill Interchange Ⓐ. Designed in the 1960s to link the M6 with the A38, a Birmingham news reporter described the plans as "cross between a plate of spaghetti and an unsuccessful attempt at a Staffordshire knot". The name Spaghetti Junction stuck and has since been applied to dozens of other motorway junctions around the world. Though futuristic at the time, the pillars support- ing the flyover had to be located carefully to avoid fouling horse-drawn canal tow ropes. Cycling beneath this monument to the motor society is an eerie and faintly dystopian experience, yet strangely peaceful.

Shortly after Spaghetti Junction, the route leaves the canal, passes back under the M6, and begins a traverse through Birmingham's northern suburbs on a string of parkland cycleways. It's pleasant enough but things get really good on entering Sutton Park. A National Nature Reserve, the park is among the largest urban green spaces in Europe, comprising open heathland, woodlands, seven lakes, wetlands and marshes. Look out for cattle and wild ponies. At the western edge of the park the route crosses one of the best-preserved Roman roads in Britain Ⓑ. This later formed the medieval highway of Icknield Street (see Ride No. 19) which ran between the Cotswolds and South Yorkshire.

After passing the suburban semis of Streetly it's a climb through farm fields to the summit of Barr Beacon Ⓒ. On the proverbial clear day, there are views across at least eleven counties and into Wales. A combination of lanes, greenways, canal towpath and riverside cycleway leads into Sandwell Valley Country Park Ⓓ. It's all very green, but this is the Black Country. Back in the 1840s it was very different, as a guidebook of the time describes: "the streams, in which no fishes swim, are black and unwholesome; the natural dead flat is often broken by high hills of cinders and spoil from the mines; the few trees are stunted and blasted; no birds are to be seen, except a few smoky sparrows; and for miles on miles a black waste spreads around, where furnaces continually smoke, steam engines thud and hiss, and long chains clank, while blind gin horses walk their doleful round."

Afer skirting around the centre of West Bromwich, the route arrives at Thomas Telford's Galton Bridge Ⓔ. Built to carry a road across a deep cutting dug for the Birmingham Canal, at the time of its construction in 1829 the cast-iron span was the highest bridge in the world. Following the canal back to the centre of Birmingham, you'll pass through the historic industrial district of Smethwick. This is where Matthew Boulton's Soho Manufactory pioneered mass production using assembly lines and where he and James Watt perfected the steam engine. The route also passes within a few hundred metres of the factory where Brooks leather saddles are made Ⓕ. Unlike once mighty Birmingham bike companies like Hercules, BSA, Phillips and Sun, Brooks is still very much in business. Likewise, Reynolds, famous for its '531' frames, is still making steel bicycle tubing across the city in Hall Green.

Arriving back into the heart of Birmingham, with its grand Victorian civic and industrial buildings augmented by a new burst of twenty-first century developments is a genuine thrill. Thanks to the canal, you can do so without having to contend with any of the city's motor traffic.

PUBS & PIT STOPS

CAFÉ PREMS, Banners Gate Entrance, Sutton Park B73 6SD (01214 390030) Small outdoor café by the children's playground.

MOCHA COFFEE LOUNGE, 8 Burnett Rd, Sutton Coldfield B74 3EJ (01213 536815) Neighbourhood coffee shop, for light bites and brunches.

PANJABI RASOI, 233 Newton Road, Great Barr B43 6HN (01213 570389) A gem of a canteen serving good value lunchtime thalis and more.

THE DISTILLERY, 4 Sheepcote Street B16 8AE (01212 002223) Canalside gin distillery and bar; look out for the Shelby's.

THE MALT HOUSE, 75 King Edwards Road B1 2NX (01216 334171) Large Greene King pub with terraces overlooking the canal.

THE FLAPPER, Cambrian Wharf B1 2NU (01212 362421) Lively bar and music venue right by the canal.

THE WELLINGTON, 37 Bennetts Hill, Birmingham B2 5SN (01212 003115) A little off-route but a good city centre pub for a post-ride pint (bring your own food or order a takeaway).

BIKE SHOPS: Bicycle Boat, Brindley Place (07547 587050) Canal boat bike workshop, behind the Sea Life Centre; Sprocket Cycles 54-57 Allison Street, Digbeth B5 5TH (01216 330730). All the main chains have city centre shops.

BIKE HIRE: Birmingham has its own town bike hire system. There's a separate folding-bike hire service run by Brompton.

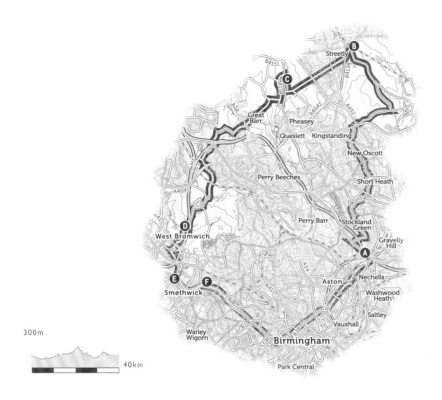

Barr Beacon

No. 19

ESCAPE VELOCITY

Straight outta B-Town to the birthplace of the Bard
and onwards to historic Warwick

———

Covering nearly 900 square miles, the West Midlands Green Belt is the size of the Peak District and the Shropshire Hills combined. It extends from Rugby in the east to Bridgnorth in the west, and from Cannock Chase in the north to Stratford-upon-Avon in the south, keeping suburban sprawl in check and providing people with precious green space. This linear route shows just how easy and satisfying it is to cycle from the city centre into the countryside and just hop on a train back.

So famous, and numerous, are Birmingham's canals, that many forget the city was founded on a river. In the centre of the city the River Rea (pronounced 'ray') is largely out of sight and out of mind: culverted beneath slabs of concrete or hidden behind high walls. But just out of the city centre, the Rea takes centre stage in a chain of parks and green spaces. The Rea Valley Cyclepath (part of National Cycle Route 5) tracks close to the river on traffic-free paths and quiet back streets. The first encounter with the river is on Longmore Street, close to Birmingham Central Mosque Ⓐ. The mosque was the second purpose-built mosque in Britain. The mosque is not allied to any one tradition of Islam but open to all; as many as 4,000 worshippers attend Friday prayers.

A little further up the river is the Edgbaston Cricket Ground, the home of the Warwickshire County side and venue for Test matches Ⓑ. The first cricket ground here was built in the 1850s, to add to the gentility of this new and upmarket suburb. Across the road from the cricket ground is Cannon Hill Park, an 80-acre landscaped pleasure garden C. The park was a gift to the city from Louisa Anne Ryland, a wealthy heiress who made dozens of gifts to the people of Birmingham, all anonymously. Among the park's more curious attractions is a scale model of the Elan Valley reservoirs which supply drinking water to Birmingham from high in Wales's Cambrian mountains, 75 miles away.

Continuing south, the Rea Valley Cyclepath passes close to Bournville, one of Birmingham's most famous districts Ⓓ. Developed from the 1880s by the Cadbury family of chocolate makers as a 'factory in a garden', it included a brand new village for Cadbury employees which would "alleviate the evils of modern, more cramped living conditions". The design of the workers' housing was traditional, taking cues from Warwickshire's black-and-white half-timbered cottages, but they came with modern interiors, unusually large gardens and were set among spacious parks and well-equipped sports grounds. Cadbury is still

START: Birmingham • FINISH: Warwick • DISTANCE: 46 miles / 74km • TOTAL ASCENT: 533m
TERRAIN: Lanes and traffic-free urban cycleways. Moderate.

Icknield Street

making chocolate in the city, though the famous Bournville dark chocolate is now made in France.

South of Bournville, the route switches from the River Rea onto the towpath of the Worcester & Birmingham Canal, following NCR 55 south. After a climb up from the canal cutting, the route joins the ancient highway of Icknield Street Ⓔ. In Roman Britain it ran from Gloucestershire to South Yorkshire and in medieval times it formed part of a route from St David's to Tynemouth.

East of Icknield Street lay the Forest of Arden, a fabled lost landscape of England. In Shakespeare's play *As You Like It*, it is to Arden that the banished Rosalind flees, dressed as a shepherd. For Shakespeare Arden represented an imagined Arcadia, as it was already much reduced by logging and land clearance. But look carefully along the field hedgerows and you will spot a few oak trees with unusually thick trunks. Could they

be the last remnants of the once-great forest? Icknield Street itself has some lovely moments running through deep, dark holloways. Just after crossing beneath the M42 the route takes in a mile of bridleway squeezed in next to the motorway. It is a dramatic juxtaposition of travel modes.

Picking a way south, the route keeps to the quietest of lanes, as far as Wilmcote. This is the village where Shakespeare's mother Mary Arden was born. Her house and the adjoining farm are run as a 'working Tudor farm', open to visitors (£) Ⓕ. From here the canal towpath offers a tranquil ride into Stratford-upon-Avon. Shakespeare was born and raised in Stratford and, though his theatrical work was all in London, he always considered Stratford to be home. Following David Garrick's Shakespeare Jubilee of 1769, the town grew into a secular shrine to the bard with all that goes with it, good and bad. More recently the town seems to have lost the battle with motor traffic. Even so, it's worth enduring the jams, the crowds, the one-way system and the tourist tat to see a performance at one of the three theatres run by the Royal Shakespeare Company.

The train from Stratford back to Birmingham is handy for evening theatre-goers, but my route continues for another 13 miles. Along the way it passes Wellesbourne airfield, a former RAF base ⓖ. A small museum tells the story of the wartime airfield, with a handful of military aircraft on show. A little further on is Charlecote Park, a very grand Elizabethan country house and landscaped grounds. Legend has it that Shakespeare was once caught poaching deer here. The estate is now run by the National Trust and open to the public (£) ⓗ. Just past Charlecote, on the way into Hampton Lucy, is Charlecote Mill, a working water mill that offers guided tours. There is a lovely wild swim spot in the River Avon a few hundred metres along a bridleway from the mill ⓘ.

The ride ends at the ancient Mercian stronghold of Warwick, with its historic town centre, excellent museum (free entry) and sensational castle (£). There is a train station for the return trip to Birmingham. If you decide to stay over, genteel Leamington Spa, the start point of Ride No. 20, is just next door.

PUBS & PIT STOPS

COACH AND HORSES INN, Weatheroak Hill, B48 7EA (01564 823386) Real ale pub that's a favourite with local cyclists. Bar food served all day.

LAMBS, 12 Sheep Street, Stratford-upon-Avon CV37 6EF (01789 292 554) Simple, well-cooked food in one of Stratford's oldest buildings. Good value set menus. Booking essential.

THE ONE ELM, 1 Guild Street, Stratford-upon-Avon CV37 6QZ (01789 404919) An interesting variety of food served at this modern pub-bistro.

TOUCHDOWN CAFÉ, Wellesbourne Airfield, Loxley Road, Wellesbourne CV35 9EU (01789 470575) Greasy spoon with an outdoor terrace looking onto the runway. Small museum tells the history of the airfield.

TWITEY'S TIPIS AND CAMPING MEADOWS, Lowe Farm, Hunscote CV35 9EX (07725 944204) Just off route, a beautiful car-free campsite with glamping options.

CHARLECOTE GARDEN CENTRE, Charlecote CV35 9ER (01789 841842) Large garden centre with a restaurant and café that's popular with local cyclists.

THE OLD POST OFFICE, 12 West Street, Warwick CV34 6AN (07796 461566) Kooky micro-pub that's perfect for a post-ride refresher.

BIKE SHOPS: Sprocket Cycles 54-57 Allison Street, Digbeth B5 5TH (01216 330730). All the main chains have shops in Birmingham city centre. The Bicycle Rooms, Unit 14, 15 Western Rd, Stratford-upon-Avon CV37 0AH (01789 414466). The Traditional Cycle Shop, Stratford Marina, Stratford-upon-Avon CV37 6YY (01789 290703).

BIKE HIRE: Stratford Bike Hire, The Stratford Greenway, Seven Meadows Rd, Old Town, Stratford-upon-Avon CV37 6GR (07711 776340).

Eastgate and St Peter's chapel, Warwick

Warwick Castle

Stratford-upon-Avon

300m

80km

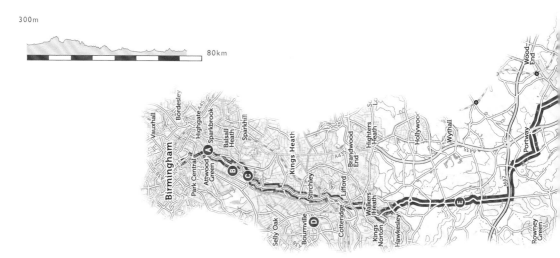

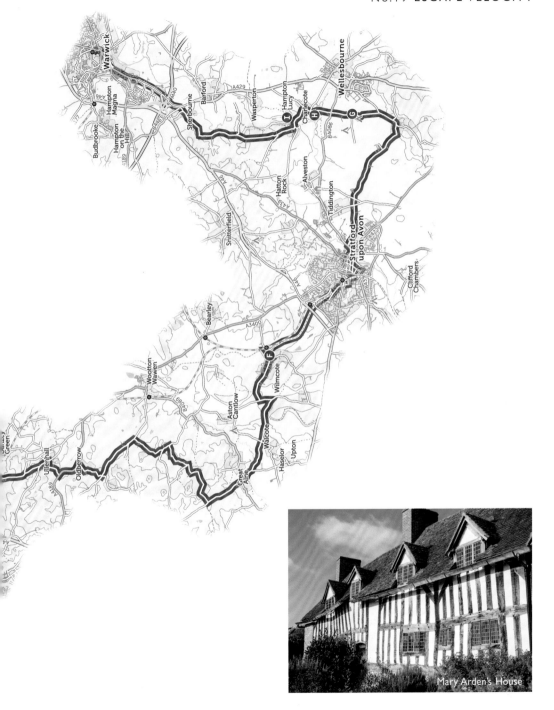

Mary Arden's House

No.20

A WARWICKSHIRE WANDER

From genteel Leamington Spa to a commanding
vantage point on the Burton Dassett hills

———

The most rural part of Warwickshire is its south, where the West Midlands green belt shades into the great diagonal stripe of limestone that extends from the Cotswolds across Northamptonshire and into Lincolnshire. This ride starts in Leamington Spa, which grew from a village of 315 people in 1801, to become a 19th century boom town thanks to the Georgian and Victorian fashion for 'taking the waters'. By 1851 it had acquired the prefix 'Royal' and had eclipsed Warwick, its ancient neighbour, to become the biggest urban area in Warwickshire after the city of Coventry. There is a drinking fountain outside the Royal Pump Rooms where you can sample the saline spring water that bubbles up from the limestone bedrock.

The ride heads out from the town centre along the River Leam (pronounced 'lem'), then the Grand Union Canal, following National Cycle Route 41 to Stockton Locks Ⓐ. This is a flight of ten locks that takes the canal up a small hill. At the top of the hill are quarries where the fossilised remains of large sea creatures have been found. They swam in a warm tropical sea over 200 million years ago, and it's the remnants of that sea that gives the spring water at Leamington Spa its salty tang. The Stockton ichthyosaur, an oversized dolphin-like creature, is on display in the Natural History Museum in London.

Napton on the Hill is a good vantage point to get a sense of the lie of the land. It was from here that army observers and local people watched the bombs rain down on Coventry on the night of the 14th November 1940, the most devastating single night of bombing of a UK city during the Second World War. Well over 500 people were killed, 43,000 homes were destroyed and swathes of the city — with its medieval centre, and its factories and workshops that were the birthplace of the modern bicycle — were reduced to rubble.

To reach the top of the hill, follow the track up to the church and continue on the path all the way to the windmill Ⓑ. The tower has been converted into a house but has retained its sails for show. 60m below, the Oxford Canal makes a circuitous loop around three sides of the hill, on its meandering course south. Built in the early years of the canal age, it is a 'contour canal', meaning it follows the lie of the land to minimise the need for costly engineering works like tunnels, cuttings and locks.

At Marston Doles the route joins Welsh Road. The name signifies that this is one of the old drover's roads, from Wales across the Midlands. It's a fabulous stretch of road to ride, only made more atmospheric by the thought of the clatter of hooves and boots, and the chatter of the drovers in their native *Cymraeg*.

START & FINISH: Leamington Spa • DISTANCE: 44 miles / 71km • TOTAL ASCENT: 532m
TERRAIN: Lanes and two shortish sections of canal towpath and bridleway. Moderate.

Grand Union Canal

A mile and a half west of Lower Boddington is the point where the counties of Worcestershire, Northamptonshire and Oxfordshire meet ⓒ. It's not just a county tripoint but a much rarer tripoint of official government regions (the West Midlands, the East Midlands and the South East). The route makes the briefest of incursions into Oxfordshire, passing through Claydon, which is home to a small 'bygones museum' of artefacts from steam engines to farm implements to household objects and shop interiors (£) ⓓ. From Claydon, a lovely farm track leads across the railway line and back into Warwickshire and the village of Farnborough. The big house of the village, Farnborough Hall, is a well-preserved Georgian country house with formal gardens set in parkland landscaped by

Sanderson Miller. He specialised in mock castles, sham ruins, towers, obelisks and other follies that seem eccentric today but were the height of fashion in Georgian England. The Holbech family gifted the estate to the National Trust in the 1960s, though they negotiated the right to continue living in the house and manage the estate. As a result, opening times are very limited (£) ⓔ.

From Farnborough it's a steady climb up the Burton Dassett hills ⓕ, a large outcrop of the same Jurassic ironstone that underlies Napton on the Hill. It's a lovely rich honey-coloured stone that has been used widely in older buildings in the area, including Farnborough Hall. After taking in the expansive views across southern Warwickshire, it's back down into the plain for the return to Leamington. Between Bishops Itchington and Harbury my route makes a short detour up to the Chesterton Windmill Ⓖ. Dating from the 1630s, the stone-built cylindrical tower mill, with an elegantly arched base, is one of Warwickshire's most famous landmarks. It's a great spot to take one last look across the landscape. To avoid the busy roads back into Leamington, the route makes use of an unsurfaced track beside the railway line

PUBS & PIT STOPS

AUBREY ALLEN, 108 Warwick Street, Leamington Spa CV32 4QP (01926 311208) Butcher and deli for superior picnic fixings.

THE STAG, Welsh Road, Offchurch CV33 9AQ (01926 425801) Smart 16th-century thatched pub serving local ales and inventive, veggie-friendly food. Terrace and garden.

THE GREEN MAN, Church Road, Long Itchington CV47 9PW (01926 812208) Village pub with no-frills camping field.

NAPTON VILLAGE STORES, New Street, Napton on the Hill CV47 8LR (01926 812488) Well-stocked village shop, deli and café.

THE FOLLY, Folly Lane, Napton on the Hill CV47 8NZ (01926 815185) Cheerful canalside inn just outside the village.

HILL FARM, Priors Hardwick CV47 7SP (07498 040602) Family farm with luxury accommodation in a shepherd's hut, a tipi and well-equipped bell tents. Traditional B&B rooms also available.

THE PLOUGH, Upper Boddington NN11 6DH (01327 260364) Thatch-roofed village pub-restaurant. Outside seating area. B&B available.

THE KITCHEN, Main Street, Farnborough, OX17 1DZ (01295 690615) Well-executed, locally-sourced food at this village pub.

THE BISHOP'S FRYER, Ladbroke Road, Bishop's Itchington CV47 2RN (01926 614093) Village chip shop, only open evenings and Friday and Saturday lunchtimes.

A few options in Harbury including the **CO-OP** for basic supplies, **THE CROWN INN**, Crown Street CV33 9HE (01926 614995) and the **SHAKESPEARE INN**, Mill Street CV33 9HR (01926 614123).

KAYAL, 42 Regent Street, Leamington Spa CV32 5EG (01926 314 800) Branch of this small Midlands chain serving Keralan food, perfect for a good value, post-ride nosh up.

THE WHITE HORSE, 4-6 Clarendon Avenue, Leamington Spa CV32 5PZ (01926 426892) Historic Victorian pub sensitively expanded into a modern bistro; hearty food served all day.

BIKE SHOPS: John Atkins Cycles, 32a Clemens Street, Leamington Spa CV31 2DN (01926 430211), Giant, 75 Clarendon Street, Leamington Spa CV32 4PW (01926 460089).

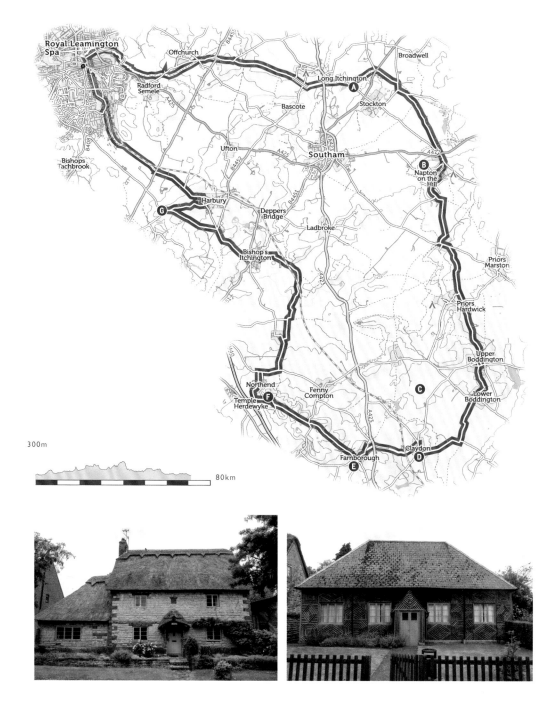

300m

80km

Chesterton windmill

Napton locks

No.21

CUT TO THE CHASE

From an ancient cathedral city to the wildness of Cannock Chase

———

With its three giant spires shooting up to the heavens and a vast, ornately statued frontage, Lichfield's cathedral makes quite an impression. For the medieval imagination it must have been overwhelming, terrifying even. In the religious turmoil of the 1500s, Christian believers whose views challenged the dominant orthodoxies were tried in the cathedral for heresy and burned alive in the Market Square. The last public execution by burning in all England took place in Lichfield in 1612. In the Civil War which followed on from the political upheavals of the Reformation, Lichfield was divided and subjected to three violent sieges. The cathedral — which Royalist forces were using as a garrison — was reduced to a wrecked shell by the Parliamentarian army.

And yet, just a few decades later, Lichfield had set aside its bloody past to become a sophisticated intellectual centre of the Enlightenment. A few hours from Birmingham, and 'just' two days from London, regular stagecoach services brought commerce and connectedness; new ideas in science, philosophy and natural history took root here and flourished. The physician and polymath Erasmus Darwin (the grandfather of Charles Darwin) hosted meetings of the Lunar Society at his house, bringing together thinkers and doers from across the Midlands. Samuel Johnson, who

was born and raised in Lichfield, declared "We are a city of philosophers. We work with our heads and let the boobies of Birmingham work for us with their hands."

From the centre of Lichfield, the ride heads out on National Cycle Route 54, passing through the construction site that will eventually create HS2, the high-speed rail line that will cut the journey time between Birmingham and Manchester to little more than 30 minutes. Back when canals were the latest thing in transport technology, such a journey would be measured not in minutes, but in days. Fradley Junction was an important interchange in the canal network and is still a popular spot for recreational boaters Ⓐ. The towpath provides a pleasant way through the village of Alrewas and over the River Trent, avoiding the shockingly poor cycle path beside the A38.

Barton-under-Needwood is the gateway to the lost forest of Needwood, originally a hunting ground for deer and wild boar and 'wood pasture' for grazing livestock and woodland crafts. In the late 1700s, the owners of the seven landed estates which owned Needwood saw the potential profits of clearing the land for modern agriculture. In an early instance of environmental protest, leading lights from Lichfield's intellectual scene including Erasmus Darwin and the Romantic poet Anna

---

START & FINISH: Lichfield • DISTANCE: 45 miles / 72km • TOTAL ASCENT: 627m
TERRAIN: Lanes and 10 miles of unpaved towpath and gravel tracks. Moderate to Challenging.

Lichfield cathedral

Seward, spoke out against the clearances. In 1808 their friend Francis Mundy published "The Fall of Needwood Forest", a poem which mourns not just the loss of nature and landscape but the loss of a traditional way of life deeply rooted in English history and folklore.

Only a few pockets of ancient woodland now remain, but nature is making a tentative return to Needwood thanks to local conservation charities. After the bridleway through Dunstall Hall, the route passes Brankley Pastures Ⓑ, where bare arable fields are being reverted to the kind of wildlife-rich 'wood pasture' that would have been typical of Needwood before the clearances. Small projects like this are part of the National Forest initiative which aspires to link the ancient forests of Needwood and Charnwood, straddling the borders of Leicestershire, Derbyshire and Staffordshire.

Across the A515, Hoar Cross Hall is another of Needwood's big estates, now a hotel and spa.

The church is a no-expense-spared mid-Victorian Gothic revival masterpiece Ⓒ. To avoid a busy main road (the B5234), my route takes a back way into Abbots Bromley. It's a well-to-do village built in Staffordshire red brick and best known, in fact world famous, for its annual Horn Dance. The ritual folk dance involves dancers bearing reindeer antlers, a man dressed as Maid Marian, a hobby horse, and a Fool. A fragment of one antler has been carbon-dated to around 1065. The dance takes place on Wakes Monday in early September but the horns are on display in the church all year round Ⓓ.

From Abbots Bromley it's south on the causeway across Blithfield Reservoir to Colton. Recrossing the Trent valley involves negotiating a mess of canal, railway and trunk roads to reach the haven of Cannock Chase. Another former royal hunting forest, it is a mixture of broadleaf woodland, coniferous plantations, open heathland, small lakes and the remains of early industries like coal mining and iron working, and a few old military training camps. With miles of good gravel tracks as well as some serious downhill trails, it's a popular local destination for mountain bikers. The main trail from the Seven Springs car park on the A513 goes up Abraham's Valley Ⓔ but you could equally well go a little to the west and ride the bridleway up the Sherbrook Valley Ⓕ, which is a little longer, a little rougher, but even more scenic. Cannock Chase is also a favourite haunt for ghost hunters and paranormal enthusiasts. Among the apparitions reportedly seen on the Chase are a pig-man, black-eyed children, werewolf-type creatures and an assortment of UFOs.

Both trails up through the Chase converge at The Butts trig point Ⓖ; from here the route heads south-east on Marquis Drive via the visitor centre Ⓗ and re-joins the tarmac road just after crossing the A460. The last few miles back to Lichfield are on pleasant country lanes. In 1834 the good people of Lichfield could choose between an incredible 72 pubs: one pub for every 69 inhabitants. The city can't match that ratio today, but it's still got far more than is usual for a place of its size. The Lichfield Real Ale Trail features traditional boozers, grand coaching inns, bistros, brew-pubs, Belgian bars, and micropubs. It's a perfect way to round off a big day out on the bike.

PUBS & PIT STOPS

FRADLEY CANALSIDE CAFÉ, Fradley Junction DE13 7DW (01283 792508) Café with outside seating by the bustling canal.

SKINNY KITTEN CAFÉ, Barton-under-Needwood DE13 8AA (01283 711217) Stylish bike-friendly café serving breakfasts, lunches & afternoon teas. Homemade cakes and scones.

THE MEYNELL INGRAM ARMS, Hoar Cross DE13 8RB (01283 575988) Large pub serving good, pub-bistro food.

Plenty of choice in Abbots Bromley, including historic inns like **THE GOATS HEAD** (07946 206322), coffee and cake at **COBWEBS**,(07966 498391), and award-winning pork pies at **THE PIE SHAK** (07962 401224), both on Goose Lane. Light bites at the **ON THE GREEN** deli-café (01283 840275).

YE OLDE DUN COW, 73 High Street, Colton WS15 3LG (01889 584026) Large country pub and B&B.

CHASE CAMPING, Four Oaks Farm, Penkridge Bank Road, WS15 2UB (01543 427977) Fun, pop-up summertime campsite set in 30 acres of open land on Cannock Chase, near the MTB trails centre

RED LION, Longdon Green WS15 4QF (01543 490410) Country pub that's a landmark with locals.

NELSON INN, Cresswell Green, Burntwood WS7 9HL (01543 674438) Handsome red brick dining pub with large garden. Food served all day.

POM'S KITCHEN AND DELI, 20-22 Bird Street, Lichfield WS13 6PR (01543 250085) Super stylish deli and coffee shop, excellent brunches.

BIKE SHOPS: Freedom Cycles, Unit 3, Windsor Business Park, Trent Valley Road, Lichfield WS13 6EU (01543 411633); Cycling 2000, 50 Wheel Lane, Lichfield WS13 7EA (01543 258280).

Sherbrook Trail

300m

80km

Abraham's Valley

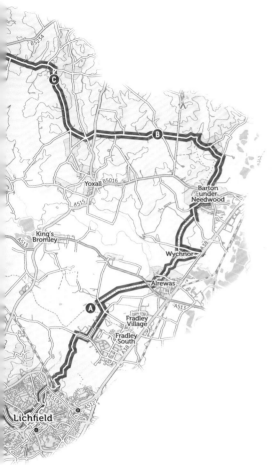

Lichfield

No. 22

GREENWOOD, GRAVEL AND GRIT

A rough-stuff adventure in the National Forest, on lanes, tracks and woodland trails

———

Unless you're already familiar with this corner of north-west Leicestershire, the sheer variety of lanes, tracks and byways on this route will come as quite a surprise. A full third of the ride is traffic-free, and most of this is on unpaved surfaces. The old adage that off-road miles count double, both in terms of time and effort, means that this is a more challenging route than its distance and elevation would imply. Splitting it over two days would allow more time to stop and explore and to add in any detours that might grab your imagination.

As befits a university town with a world-class reputation in sport, exercise and engineering, Loughborough has a better-than-average network of cycle routes. The ride begins on National Cycle Route 6 to Shepshed, first on suburban streets then onto some traffic-free farm tracks to a bridge over the M1 motorway. Quiet lanes through Belton lead straight to the ruins of Grace Dieu Priory Ⓐ. The nunnery was founded in 1239 by Roesia de Verdun, a member of the Anglo-Norman landowning gentry. By all accounts a powerful, independent and fearless woman, after her husband's death she sought to avoid having to marry again, and therefore risk losing her wealth and disinheriting her children. Becoming a nun was a surefire way of doing this. Her remains lie

in Belton village church. Today, the atmospheric ruins of Grace Dieu are a favourite haunt of ghost hunters. In just one dusk-to-dawn vigil, members of Leicestershire Paranormal Association observed a spectral banquet, a young boy playing a flute, a drummer boy, three soldiers being executed, horses pulling carts loaded with barrels, and assorted farm animals. When Henry VIII brought an abrupt end to monastic life in England in the 1530s it would be three hundred years until another permanent monastery was founded, just a few miles east of Grace Dieu, at Mount St Bernard Ⓑ. In 2018, its monks became the first in the Britain to brew Trappist beer, a delicious strong brown ale at a punchy 7.5% alcohol.

A forest track leads to the village of Whitwick, and onwards into Coalville. A supermarket now stands on the site of the Whitwick colliery, the first in the area, sunk in the 1820s. Coalville itself was founded soon after, with the coming of the railways and other industries to the area, and grew into one of Leicestershire's biggest towns. The 1980s saw the closure of the last six mines, when around 5,000 men lost their jobs. The site of Snibston colliery is now a country park with mountain bike trails and a nature reserve Ⓒ. Some of the mining and railway equipment has been preserved but sadly a popular museum devoted to

START & FINISH: Loughborough • DISTANCE: 45 miles / 72km • TOTAL ASCENT: 645m
TERRAIN: Lanes, cycleways and 15 miles of unpaved tracks, a few of
which are rough and can be muddy when wet. Challenging.

The Battlefield Line

Shackerstone station tea rooms

Snibston colliery

science and industry was demolished in 2016 due to lack of funds.

Beyond Ravenstone, the route passes between the sites of two former open cast coal mines undergoing landscape transformation. On the left is the 150-acre Sence Valley Forest Park, on the right is the 460-acre Queen Elizabeth Diamond Jubilee Wood. The latter's 300,000 saplings will grow into one of the single largest expanses of woodland of the National Forest, an ambitious plan to connect the ancient medieval forests of Charnwood and Needwood.

The road follows the River Sence downhill as far as Shackerstone. It's an idyllic spot — people messing about on boats on the canal, and steam trains huffing and puffing along the Battlefield

Line. Shackerstone station is an exquisitely maintained relic of the bygone age of steam, complete with a small museum and a lovely Victorian tearoom ⒟. From here trains run five miles south to Shenton, close to Bosworth Field, the site of the final battle of the Wars of the Roses in which Richard III was defeated and killed, marking the start of a new dynasty under Henry Tudor.

Heading eastwards, the route climbs through the hamlet of Barton in the Beans, originally denoting a barley farm where beans are also grown. The beans in question are broad beans, also known as fava beans (there is a similarly named village in Nottinghamshire called Barton in Fabis). Broad beans were once a staple food crop, and the saying goes "shake a Leicestershire man by the collar and you may hear the beans rattle in his belly". A pearl of a green lane (named, appropriately enough, Green Lane) leads to some forest trails through Grange Wood. This is all part of National Cycle Route 63, but it is not well sign-posted and requires careful navigation.

Burroughs Wood is at the western end of a chain of woodland that leads across the M1 to Groby (pronounced "Groo-bee"), a once a medieval manor that's now a residential suburb of Leicester. After passing the still waters of Groby Pool, it's more traffic-free miles through Bradgate Park. Set in a deer park on the edge of the Charnwood Forest, Bradgate House is a once-magnificent Tudor mansion that now stands in ruins Ⓔ. It was the childhood home of Lady Jane Grey, a cousin of King Edward VI. Upon the death of the teenage king in 1553 Lady Jane was declared queen, in large part as a means of keeping the crown in Protestant hands. After just nine days she was overthrown by the supporters of Edward's Catholic half-sister Mary Tudor. Convicted of treason, Lady Jane was beheaded at the age of just 17.

Yet more forest trails lead through Swithland Wood Ⓕ. It is one of the best remnants of native woodland in Leicestershire and especially noted for its carpets of bluebells in spring. Following the road through upmarket Woodhouse Eaves, there is a final helping of gravel on the lane to Woodthorpe, from where the route joins the cycleways on the main roads back into Loughborough.

PUBS & PIT STOPS

COLLIERY CAFÉ, Ashby Road, Coalville LE67 3LN (01163 058190) Modern café on the site of the old Snibston colliery, now a country park.

CATTOWS FARM, Swepstone Road, Heather LE67 2RF (01530 264200) Farm shop and café, a mile off route.

THE BELPER ARMS, Newton Burgoland LE67 2SE (01530 886537) Oldest pub in Leicestershire which retains a good deal of its charm. ¾ mile off route.

HELP OUT MILL, Heather Road, near Shackerstone, CV13 0BT (01530 260666) Restaurant in a grand old watermill (Friday-Sunday only, booking recommended).

THE RISING SUN, Church Road, Shackerstone CV13 6NN (01827 880215) Village pub. Food at weekends.

VICTORIAN TEA ROOMS, Shackerstone Station CV13 6NW (07950 512587) Lovingly maintained vintage tearooms on the platform of the Battlefield Line heritage steam railway.

THE BRICKLAYERS ARMS, 213 Main Street, Thornton LE67 1AH (01530 230808) Friendly village pub with decent pub classics from the kitchen.

THE WHEATSHEAF INN, Brand Hill, Woodhouse Eaves LE12 8SS (01509 890320) Heavily made-over former slate workers pub; plenty of outside seating.

BIKE SHOP: Cycle-Trax, 214 Park Road, Loughborough LE11 2HJ (01509 233532), Pedal Power, 5 Ashby Rd, Loughborough LE11 3AA (01509 269663).

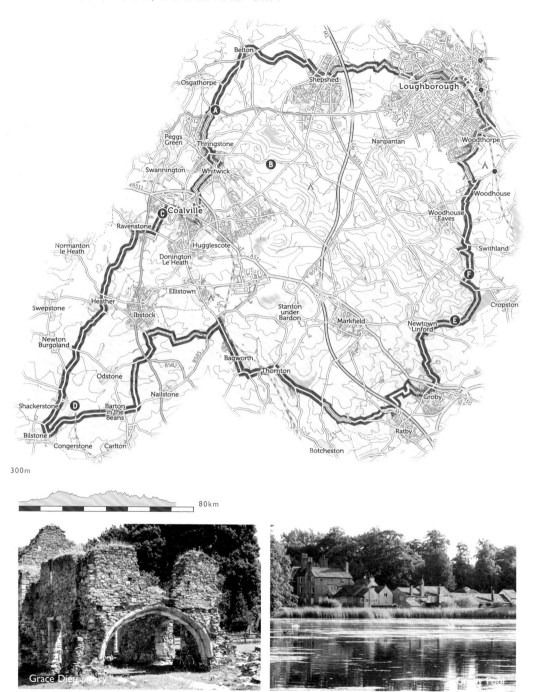

300m

80km

Grace Dieu priory

Bradgate House

TO THE MANOR BORN

A stately circuit of the gently rolling county of 'spires and squires'

———

The county of Northamptonshire has one of England's highest concentrations of stately homes. The expression of power and money displayed by these landmarks show them as repositories of history and culture; yet they often also stand as monuments to the ill-gotten gains of feudalism, colonialism and imperialism. They can provide really good places to ride a bike, with quiet lanes and traffic-free byways through beautifully landscaped parkland, but they can also be walled-off fiefdoms from which time-worn public rights of way have been extinguished. However you look at the country's landed estates, it's important to do so in the round. This ride takes in five of them, connected by some choice lanes and byways.

From the centre of Northampton, the route heads north on the Brampton Valley Way, a traffic-free trail along the route of an old railway line. It's possible to ride all the way to Market Harborough but the route turns off just outside Brixworth. If you've an interest in historic architecture then you'll want to make the short detour up the hill to Brixworth to see the Saxon church Ⓐ. Built in part-recycled Roman masonry, it's not just the largest substantially intact Saxon church in England, but probably the largest building of any kind from this period.

A few miles on is Cottesbrooke Hall, built in 1702 for the descendants of the merchant and politician Sir John Langham, who made a fortune as a prominent member of the Levant and East India Companies, at the time when England was emerging as a global naval power. The 13-acre garden is 20th century Arts and Crafts with mid-century work by Geoffrey Jellicoe and Sylvia Crowe and plantings by contemporary designers Arne Maynard and James Alexander-Sinclair (£, RHS members free) Ⓑ.

It's then a climb up to the crossing of the A14 at Naseby. From this ridge, on a foggy June morning in 1645, the New Model Army of Oliver Cromwell faced the main Royalist army of King Charles I, which was lined up a mile or two to the north Ⓒ. The Royalist army was routed, bringing an end to any chance of resisting the Parliamentarians' ultimate victory.

The next great house on the route is Stanford Hall, built in 1697 by the same architect as Cottesbrooke. Stanford very nearly secured a place in modern history when, in 1899, aviation pioneer Percy Pilcher set about testing his new engine-powered triplane. Days before the planned flight the engine crankshaft broke, so Pilcher chose to fly his unpowered glider instead. Wet weather caused the glider's tail to snap and Pilcher fell

START & FINISH: Northampton • DISTANCE: 48 miles / 77km • TOTAL ASCENT: 678m
TERRAIN: Lanes, some urban roads and 7 miles of unpaved cycleways and byways. Moderate.

Ashby Manor House

to his death before he had the chance to see if his triplane could fly. This was four years before the Wright brothers' first powered flight at Kitty Hawk. There is a memorial to Pilcher's exploits in a field on the left of the road Ⓓ. Look out too for fields of 'ridge and furrow' created by repeated ploughing in the medieval open-field system of agriculture.

Topographical and historical destiny draws the route towards the Watford Gap, a narrow pass between two hill systems into which are squeezed Watling Street (the Roman road that's now the A5), the Grand Union Canal, the West Coast mainline railway, and the M1. Linguists have identified the Watford Gap as marking the divide between the dialects of northern England

and southern England. It is also very nearly on Britain's east-west watershed: one nearby river flows east to the North Sea and another west to the Irish Sea. Opened in 1959, the Blue Boar at Watford Gap was Britain's first service station. It soon became a legendary late-night hangout for musicians on the road. The Beatles, the Rolling Stones, the Eagles, Pink Floyd, Dusty Springfield and James Brown are all known to have rocked up at its formica tables.

After crossing the M1 by bridge, a quiet lane leads to Ashby St Ledgers. It was here, in the half-timbered gatehouse of his family manor, that Robert Catesby hatched a terrorist plot to blow up Parliament, kill the Protestant king and install a Catholic in his place Ⓔ. Popular retellings of the story cast Guy Fawkes as the chief villain — it was Fawkes who was caught red-handed with the 36 barrels of gunpowder — but there is no doubt that Catesby was the mastermind. From just south of the village of Norton, a sublime wooded bridleway crosses the railway, the canal and back over the motorway, emerging into the landscaped parkland of Brockhall Hall Ⓕ. Dating from the early 1600s, the manor house is now divided into apartments. A superb gravel track leads up to Little Brington and into the orbit of Althorp, the final and grandest of the ride's great estates.

The Spencer family rose to prominence and exceptional wealth in Elizabethan England due to their success as sheep farmers. Astute in business, politics and in marriage within the nobility, the wealth of the Spencers grew and grew.

Literary, arty and socially flamboyant, liberal-leaning Spencers championed progressive causes including political reform, the abolition of slavery and Irish Home Rule. Elaborate memorials in the church at Great Brington mark the burial places of generations of Spencers [G], though the most famous Spencer of all, Diana, Princess of Wales, is buried in the grounds of the house. Her specially constructed mausoleum is on an island in a lake which, according to her younger brother Charles Spencer who lives at Althorp, acts "as a buffer against the interventions of the insane and ghoulish". The house and grounds, though not Diana's mausoleum, are open to visitors in summer (£) Ⓗ. The last miles back through the suburban outskirts of Northampton are efficient, if lacking the splendour of the rest of the ride.

PUBS & PIT STOPS

OLD VICARAGE TEAROOMS, Church St, Naseby NN6 6DA (01604 740302) Uniquely homely tearoom. Sundays only, except by arrangement.

SQUISITO, 46 The High Street, Yelvertoft NN6 6LQ (07544 428165) Village butchers reborn as a deli, cheese shop, cookery school and more.

THE ROYAL OAK, 22 Church St, Crick NN6 7TP (01788 822340) Village pub with a curry-heavy food menu.

PICKLE AND PIE, 23 Church St, Crick NN6 7TP (01788 823579) Outstanding hot lunches, coffee and more.

THE WHITE HORSE, 51 Daventry Rd, Norton NN11 2ND (01327 702982) Friendly, unfussy pub serving good beer, fish and chips next door.

ALTHORP COACHING INN, Main Street, Great Brington NN7 4JA (01604 770651) Oak beams, snug alcoves, log fires, and good ales and food. Pub heaven.

BIKE SHOPS: Velo Haus, 1 Gold Street Mews, Northampton NN1 1RA (01604 947914); Cycle King, 208-210 Kettering Road, Northampton NN1 4BN (01604 232221).

BIKE HIRE: Rutland Cycling, Pitsford Water, Brixworth Country Park NN6 9DG (01604 881 777).

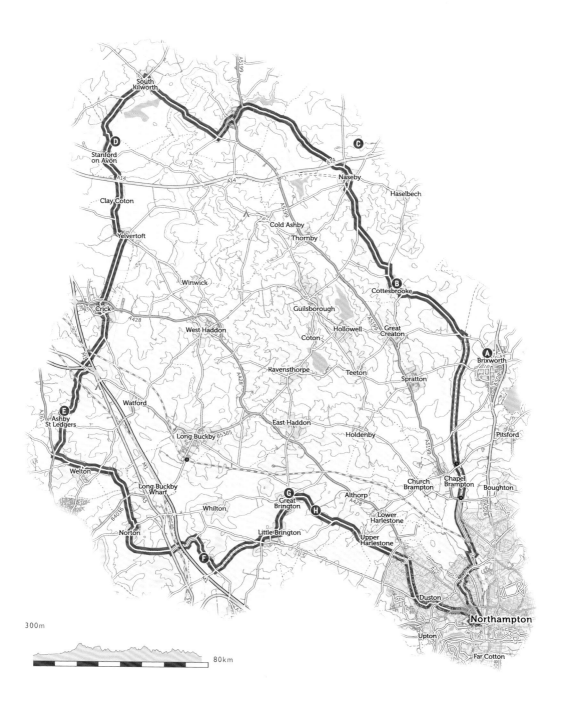

300m

80km

Brixworth church

EAST MIDLANDS

No.24

SMALL IS BEAUTIFUL

Across Rutland to the Rockingham Forest
and the haunting ruins of Fotheringhay Castle

It's said that good things come in small packages or, as the Rutland county motto puts it, *Multum in Parvo*, literally 'much in little' or, perhaps more poetically, 'there's more than meets the eye'. What the smallest of England's 39 historic counties lacks in acreage it makes up for in the sheer variety of landscapes, from the shimmering expanse of Rutland Water, the second largest body of water in England after Windermere, to some decidedly lumpy terrain in the south of the county. This route starts and finishes in Oakham but riding just the loop from the southern lakeshore reduces the total distance by about ten miles.

Rutland's county emblem is a horseshoe, a nod to an Oakham custom dating back to the Norman conquest that required visiting bigwigs to forfeit a horseshoe to the lord of the manor. Over time, these became increasingly large and ornate. More than two hundred now hang in the great hall of the castle (entry is free) Ⓐ. The castle itself is no more, but its earthen ramparts offer a good view across the town's rooftops.

A signed roadside cycleway connects Oakham with the 17-mile traffic-free cycle trail around Rutland Water. The reservoir was created in the 1970s by flooding the valley of the River Gwash with water from the Rivers Welland and Nene. At first, local people vigorously opposed the plan.

They must have felt under siege as they were simultaneously contending with the abolition of Rutland as a county and its absorption into Leicestershire. In the decades since, the reservoir has become a major attraction for fishing, sailing, cycling, bird watching and walking. Rutland was re-established as a county in 1997.

The route follows the reservoir's perimeter cycleway anti-clockwise, including a detour up the hill to Manton, to skirt around a nature reserve, as far as the village of Edith Weston. This is a curious name: sadly the Edith in question isn't the long-serving village postmistress, but Edith of Wessex, the last Saxon queen of England. Here the route heads south from Rutland Water, but it's worth riding on just half a mile to see Normanton church, possibly Rutland's most famous landmark Ⓑ. The classically styled church was set to be lost beneath the reservoir's rising waters but, following an outcry, was saved - the lower levels were filled with rubble, and a causeway and dyke were built around the church to prevent it dissolving.

After crossing the gentle valleys of the Chater and the Welland, the route leaves Rutland for Northamptonshire and the remnants of Rockingham Forest. Once a royal hunting ground that stretched from Stamford to Northampton, forest rule meant that only the king could hunt

START & FINISH: Oakham • DISTANCE: 51 miles / 82km • TOTAL ASCENT: 751m
TERRAIN: Mostly lanes with 9 miles of unpaved lakeside and forest tracks. Moderate to Challenging.

deer and wild boar, and the clearance of land for farming and fuel was not allowed. In the 18th and 19th centuries, though, most of the trees was felled and the land enclosed for grazing. A few pockets of ancient woodland remain, often coppiced. Fineshade Wood is a large woodland that is managed for public access. A good gravel track leads to the village of King's Cliffe.

Beyond King's Cliffe, the next few miles are a delight for architectural historians. Apethorpe (pronounced 'Apthorpe') is a pretty village built around Apethorpe Palace, one of England's grandest country houses, recently rescued from dereliction and open to the public for a limited number of days each year (English Heritage, £) ©. The church at Nassington contains the remains of a Saxon stone cross, some great medieval wall paintings and a clock mechanism dating from 1695 (there's another by the same maker at the church in Apethorpe).

These are just preludes to the main event. To describe Fotheringhay as a ruined castle is to exaggerate what are just a few earthen mounds. But once you know something of its history, and tune in to the powerful *genius loci*, you cannot help but be captivated. A royal stronghold dating back to 1100, the castle was home to the Dukes of York, one side in the protracted and bloody civil war now known by the somewhat sugarcoated name 'Wars of the Roses'. Richard III was born here and the parish church is packed with Plantagenet and Yorkist relics. The Tudor monarchs deliberately let the castle go, downgrading Fotheringhay to the status of a state prison. After Mary, Queen of Scots was implicated (probably falsely) in a plot to assassinate Elizabeth I and take the crown for herself, she was brought here, tried for treason and beheaded. The choice of location was surely not coincidental. The castle was left to decay completely and locals plundered the masonry. It remains a beautiful and, at times, melancholic spot on a slight rise above the meandering River Nene Ⓓ.

A little way down the River Nene is Oundle, a smart town of handsome stone buildings and a famous private school. From here the route turns north for the return journey on quiet lanes through the vast arable fields that now occupy what was once the heart of Rockingham Forest. It's simple, pleasant riding. Immediately after crossing back into Rutland comes another scenic highlight of the route, the Welland Viaduct Ⓔ. This is the longest masonry viaduct across a valley anywhere in the UK — its 82 arches required a total of 30 million bricks. The viaduct is another feather in the cap of little Rutland. The best view of it in the late afternoon light is from the lane to Seaton, though you will need to find a hole in the hedge to get into the adjacent field. A few more miles of rolling lanes lead back to Manton and the lakeside cycleway back to Oakham.

PUBS & PIT STOPS

HORSE AND JOCKEY INN, St Marys Road, Manton LE15 8SU (01572 737335) First and last pub on this route; small campsite at the back.

BARROWDEN AND WAKERLEY COMMUNITY SHOP, 22 Wakerley Road, Barrowden LE15 8EP (01572 748748) Shop and café serving light lunches and home-made cakes. Outside seating area.

KINGS CLIFFE BAKERY, 68 West Street, Kings Cliffe PE8 6XA (01780 470205) Local landmark bakery and cafe, closes 1pm.

CROSS KEYS, 2 West Street, King's Cliffe PE8 6XA (01780 470030) Dining pub in an 18th century building with ales from the brewery in the village.

WILLOW AND BROOK, Apethorpe PE8 5DG (01780 470509) Popular pub-restaurant with good vegan and gluten-free options.

ELSIE'S VINTAGE TEA ROOM, Nassington PE8 6QG (01780 783313) Fabulously kooky tea rooms.

CASTLE FARM CAMPSITE, Fotheringhay PE8 5HZ (07976 958452) Tranquil riverside campsite beneath the castle ruins. Bell tents available.

Plenty of choice in Oundle. Try the **TAP AND KITCHEN,** Oundle Wharf PE8 4DE (01832 275069) down by the river, **BREWBABU,** 6 West Street PE8 4EF (01832 273909) and **BEANS COFFEE SHOP,** 1 New St PE8 4EA (01832 270007) in the centre of town.

BULWICK VILLAGE STORES, 15 Main St, Bulwick NN17 3DY (01780 450774) Outstanding village shop, deli and café with an outside terrace. Breakfasts, lunches and afternoon teas.

GEORGE AND DRAGON, 2 Main Street, Seaton LE15 9HU (01572 747418) Smart gastropub, B&B available.

THE OLD PHEASANT HOTEL, 15 Main Road, Glaston LE15 9BP (01572 822326) Large country pub-hotel, bar billiards.

BIKE SHOPS: Giant Store Rutland, Normanton Car Park, Edith Weston LE15 8HD (01780 720888): bike hire available. Sigma Sports, The Old Mill Yard, South Street, Oakham LE15 6HY (0333 006 8833). Oakham Cycle Centre, 2 Barleythorpe Road, Oakham LE15 6NR (01572 757058); also bike hire.

BIKE HIRE: Grounds Cycle Centre, Fineshade Wood NN17 3BB (07888 441564) Cycle hire, workshop and café.

Normanton church

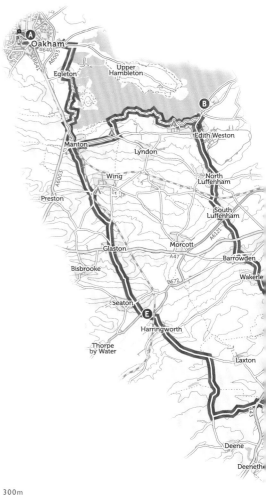

300m

100km

River Nene

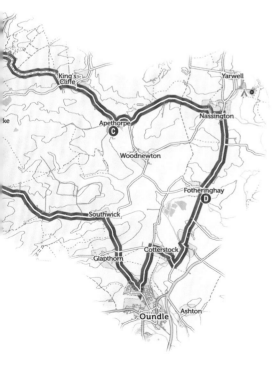

King's Cliffe

Yarwell

Apethorpe

C

Nassington

Woodnewton

Fotheringhay

D

Southwick

Cotterstock

Glapthorn

Oundle

Ashton

Fotheringhay church

HIGHER GROUND

The quiet lanes and gated roads of High Leicestershire are a cycling paradise

——

This ride will refute any misguided idea that Leicestershire is flat. 'High' Leicestershire is the diamond-shaped area between Melton Mowbray in the north, Market Harborough in the south, Leicester in the west and Rutland Water in the east. It's a landscape of broad, rolling ridges and secluded valleys. The atmosphere is rural and remote. The villages are small and the scattered farms combine grazing pasture on the hilltops with arable crops on the lower, flatter fields. What makes the area especially good for cycling, however, is the network of narrow country lanes, many of them with gates you have to open and close as you go, a feature which puts off almost all motorists who don't actually live there. Added to this is a greater density of traffic-free bridleways and byways than is found elsewhere in England, where many such old ways are classified as footpaths, and therefore not welcoming to cyclists.

The route begins in Melton Mowbray, a foodie town famous for pork pies and Stilton cheese. It's worth packing a picnic for this ride as the remoteness of High Leicestershire means there is only a handful of places to stop for lunch on the route. Heading due south from the town centre, the route starts out as it means to continue, on a gem of a gated lane, heading straight for Burrough Hill, one of the highest points in the county, and the location of a major Iron Age hill fort Ⓐ. It returns via the summit of the hill on the return leg. South of the village of Burrough on the Hill there are more choice gated lanes via Newbold and Owston. It's not the most direct route, but that's not really the point of this kind of ride.

This pleasantly meandering course leads to Launde Abbey, a former monastic house tucked away in the gently sheltered combe of the River Chater Ⓑ. It is a spot so beautiful, that Thomas Cromwell, chief advisor to Henry VIII, earmarked Launde for himself as a country estate where he might retire and grow old. Among his many responsibilities, Cromwell instigated and oversaw the task of disbanding and sale of hundreds of wealthy monastic houses, seen as corrupt nests of superstition that were holding the country back. Confiscating fine monastic houses, extensive lands and all the wealth that came with it was an added bonus for the cash-strapped monarch. As Henry's right hand man, Cromwell would have had his pick of the best estates.

Intelligent, worldly, hardworking, cunning, successful yet ultimately tragic, Thomas Cromwell is one of the most compelling figures in English history. His retirement to Launde was never to be. A sudden and spectacular fall from favour saw him executed for treason.

START & FINISH: Melton Mowbray • DISTANCE: 34 miles / 55km • TOTAL ASCENT: 710m
TERRAIN: Lanes and 2 miles of unpaved rural byways. Moderate.

Launde Abbey

Cromwell's story is retold and reimagined in Hilary Mantel's glittering *Wolf Hall* trilogy. Cromwell's son Gregory lived at Launde for a decade until his death at 31 from the sweating sickness, a mysterious contagion that was rife in the Tudor era. And perhaps the medieval monks of Launde have had the last laugh — today the house is run as a Christian retreat centre. The gardens are open to patrons of its café.

Beyond Launde are more superb lanes and traffic-free byways, crossing over into Rutland and a trio of attractive ironstone villages - Belton, Brooke and Braunston. All three have 12th century churches worth a stop, but especially Brooke, whose Elizabethan oak interior furnishings led to the church's inclusion in the poet John Betjeman's list of the top 100 churches in England Ⓒ.

It's a gradual climb from Braunston to Somersby, whose village pub, The Stilton Cheese Inn, dates back to 1666. It regularly features in lists of the best pubs in Leicestershire. It's a good stop for refreshments before continuing to the entrance to Burrough Hill Ⓐ. This large hill fort, built on a natural promontory of Jurassic ironstone, is one of the best sunset viewpoints in the East Midlands. Archeological digs have found material from the early Bronze Age continuing well into the Roman period. Among the many finds are spearheads, knives, hooks and tools associated with metalworking, weaving, spinning, pottery and other domestic and craft activities. The plateau within the ramparts would have been occupied by timber roundhouses.

There is an ancient trackway straight from the fort to Melton Mowbray, and it is still possible to ride it today, though the first part is steep and loose — so definitely a rough-stuff option.

Instead, my route retraces the road back through Burrough on the Hill and picks up the trackway at the foot of the hill Ⓓ. It's now a byway and, though undoubtedly rustic, is completely passable. The last miles back to Melton follow the same glorious gated road as at the start of the ride, and it's no hardship to ride it one more time.

PUBS & PIT STOPS

YE OLDE PORK PIE SHOPPE, 10 Nottingham Street, Melton Mowbray LE13 1NW (01664 562341) The oldest bakers of the celebrated pork pies; try also the fruit-filled Melton Hunt Cake.

VINE FARM DAIRY MILK SHED, Top End, Great Dalby LE14 2HA. Innovative 'honesty box' shack serving fresh milk, hot drinks, milkshakes and cakes.

THE STAG AND HOUNDS, 4 Main St, Burrough on the Hill, LE14 2JQ (01664 454250) Fine dining restaurant and pub, with a good lighter bites menu for travellers.

THE OLD STABLES, Manor Farm House, 18 Main St, Burrough on the Hill LE14 2JQ (01664 454468) B&B well located for Burrough hill fort and the Stag and Hounds restaurant (above).

CAFÉ VENTOUX, Wood Lane, Tugby LE7 9WE (01162 598063) Three miles off-route, a popular cycling-themed café-bar that serves good, freshly-prepared food and hosts a season of bike events. Also sells basic spares for repairs.

LAUNDE ABBEY CAFÉ, Launde Abbey LE7 9XB (01572 717254) Café in the Christian education centre serving morning coffees, light snacks and (booking required) afternoon teas and Sunday roasts.

THE BLUE BALL, Braunston LE15 8QS (01572 722135) This 17th century thatched inn claims to be the oldest in Rutland. Cosy in winter with lots of outside seating for summer months.

FOX AND HOUNDS, Knossington LE15 8LY (01664 452129) Homely food-oriented country pub, booking advised.

THE STILTON CHEESE INN, High Street, Somerby LE14 2PZ (01664 454394) Popular real ale pub serving the usual pub fayre.

BIKE SHOP: Halfords, Norman Way, Snow Hill, Melton Mowbray LE13 1JE (01664 566923). See also Café Ventoux, above.

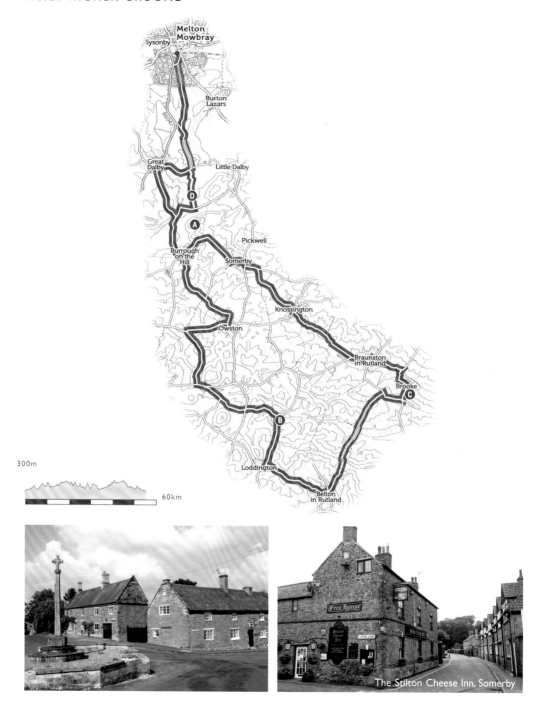

300m

60km

The Stilton Cheese Inn, Somerby

View from Burrough Hill

THE FAT OF THE LAND

From the home of the pork pie to the land of Stilton cheese,
on quiet lanes, tracks and byways

———

Starting out of Melton Mowbray, the route heads north on National Cycle Route 64 through Melton Country Park. Then a gentle climb into the Leicestershire Wolds, a limestone escarpment which overlooks the flatlands of Nottinghamshire. To avoid the motor traffic on the main ridge road along the top of the wolds, my route follows quiet lanes through the attractive villages of Eaton and Branston before heading off-road onto a lovely wooded bridleway along the Terrace Hills. From here there are some big views over the Vale of Belvoir Ⓐ.

The Vale takes its name from Belvoir Castle, originally a Norman stronghold that became the ancestral home of the Dukes of Rutland. Belvoir, meaning Beautiful View in the French of the conquering Normans, is pronounced 'beaver' - supposedly because the local Anglo-Saxon population didn't speak the language of their new feudal masters. At any rate, the castle is aptly named, as it does indeed command a beautiful view. There are, as far as we know, no beavers in the area.

The present castle is the fourth on the site, a 19th century fantasy of turrets and battlements that doubled for Windsor Castle in the hit TV series The Crown. It's said that the middle- and upper-class English ceremony of 'afternoon tea' was invented here in the 1840s, by the Duchess

of Bedford, to bridge the gap between the lunch at midday and evening meal. The present Duke, whose wealth is reckoned to be £145 million, was a high-profile supporter of the UK Independence Party. Belvoir Castle and its grounds are open to the public (£) Ⓑ.

The church in the large village of Bottesford is the parish church of Belvoir Castle; assorted lords of the manor are entombed beneath elaborate memorials. On one of these, witchcraft is cited as the cause of death of two young heirs to the lordship, an accusation that led to the deaths of two almost certainly innocent women who worked at the castle. More happily, the church is now home to a family of peregrine falcons, nesting in the tower.

On the way out of Bottesford the route passes Belvoir Fruit Farm, producers of high-end fruit cordials Ⓒ. It all started back in 1984 when Lady Mary Manners, aunt of the current Duke of Rutland, made a thousand bottles of her home-made elderflower cordial. Now run by Lady Mary's son, Belvoir Farm presently employs over 50 people, making 25 million bottles a year, exported worldwide. Elderflower remains the mainstay; harvesting the flower heads in late May and early June is a major event. A small army of harvesters pick the farm's own 60-acre plantation but fans out across the Vale to forage flowers from

---

START & FINISH: Melton Mowbray • DISTANCE: 46 miles / 74km • TOTAL ASCENT: 553m
TERRAIN: Lanes and 6 miles of unpaved canal towpath and bridleways. Easy.

Bottesford ford

gardens and hedgerows. In 2021 the going rate was £2.70/kg.

There are some excellent rough stuff byways in the Vale that are well worth exploring, but the route sticks to quiet lanes via Plungar, Granby and Langar. From here a gated lane leads directly to the creamery at Colston Bassett, one of three producers of Stilton cheese in the Vale. On the lane out of the village look out for the eerie ruins of St Mary's church, accessible down a short track Ⓓ.

Soon after Colston Bassett it's onto the towpath of the Grantham Canal. For a brief time, this was the chief artery of the area, transporting ironstone mined in the Wolds to the forges at Nottingham. They would return loaded with foul-smelling cargoes of 'night soil' from the city's privies and pisspots to spread on the fields as fertiliser.

Along the way you'll pass an avenue of poplar trees on the left Ⓔ. The trees are a living memorial to the 184 men of the Sherwood Foresters who were killed in the Battle of Vimy Ridge in northern France during the First World War. It was the initiative of Jesse Hind, a solicitor from Nottingham whose only son was among the men killed. Hind also bought the farm at the far end of the track, renamed it Vimy Ridge Farm, and established it as an agricultural training centre for returning soldiers and local destitute orphans. The farm now stands in ruins, almost as if it has been transplanted from among the wreckage of the Western Front.

The route leaves the towpath at the canal basin at Hickling Ⓕ. Local children have long been told the story of the huge whale which comes along the canal from Grantham at midnight to turn around in the basin. The churchyard at Hickling is a good place to find 'Belvoir angels', intricately carved motifs on gravestones from the period 1690 to 1760. None of them are pretty, some sinister, all different. There are more in the churchyard at Nether Broughton Ⓖ.

From here it's a short climb up the steeper scarp slope of the Wolds. The final miles back to Melton Mowbray are on a good track and farm lanes through the parish of Ab Kettleby, a quiet rural backwater with some distinctive buildings made from the rich, orangey-yellow local ironstone. Look out for a small church that looks out of place, with no settlement nearby Ⓗ. This is the last remaining building of Welby, a medieval village, where a local farmer discovered a hoard of Bronze Age metal objects in a field. That which wasn't melted down is on display at the Melton Carnegie Museum.

PUBS & PIT STOPS

YE OLDE PORK PIE SHOPPE, 10 Nottingham Street, Melton Mowbray LE13 1NW (01664 562341) The oldest bakers of the celebrated pork pies; try also the fruit-filled Melton Hunt Cake.

CAFÉ ALLEZ!, visitor car park, Belvoir Castle NG32 1PE (07786 854794) Tiny cycling-themed coffee stop.

CHEQUERS INN, Woolsthorpe by Belvoir NG32 1LU (01476 870701) Quintessential English country pub, food served all day, rooms available.

THE DIRTY DUCK, Woolsthorpe Wharf, NG32 1NY (01476 870111) Canalside pub with a large beer garden. Campsite next door.

PAUL'S, 1 Market St, Bottesford NG13 0BW (01949 842375) Top notch bistro for a long, lazy lunch.

BOTTESFORD FISH AND CHIP BAR, 3 Queen Street, Bottesford NG13 0AH (01949 843187) Chippy open lunchtimes Wed-Sat.

DICKIES FARM DINING, Orchard Farm, 45 Barkestone Lane, Plungar NG13 0JA (01949 869733) Seriously good meat in a rustic tin-roofed shack. Evenings and Sunday lunch only, booking essential. Shepherds' huts next door for overnight stays.

NATURESCAPE WILDFLOWER FARM, Coach Gap Lane, Langar NG13 9HP (01949 860592) Tea room on a wildflower farm.

COLSTON BASSETT DAIRY, Harby Lane, Colston Bassett NG12 3FN (01949 81322) Stilton cheese straight from the source.

THE MARTIN'S ARMS, School Lane, Colston Bassett NG12 3FD (01949 81361) Widely acclaimed dining pub.

THROUGH THE GATE CAFÉ, Nether Broughton LE14 3ES (07976 409923) Just off-route, a good-value farm cafe with venison and bison from their own herds.

NICE PIE, Six Hills Lane, Old Dalby LE14 3NB (07531 641893) Just off-route, a tearoom and farm shop selling award-winning pies.

BIKE SHOP: Halfords, Norman Way, Snow Hill, Melton Mowbray LE13 1JE (01664 566923).

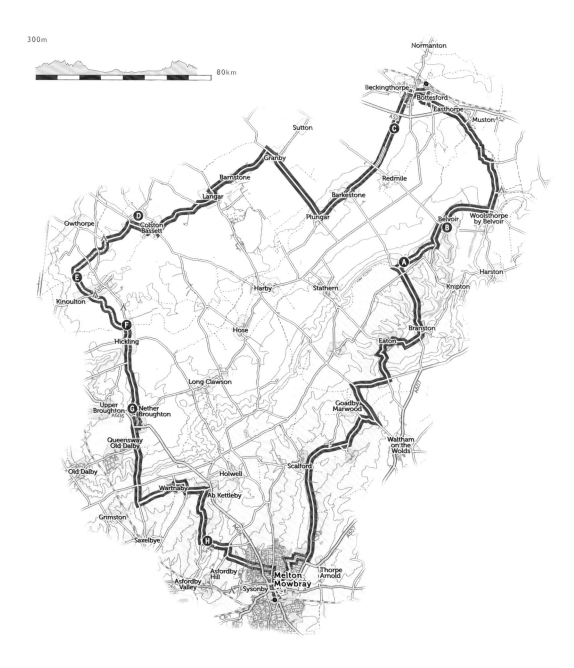

300m

80km

Normanton

Beckingthorpe
Bottesford
Easthorpe
Muston

Sutton

C

Granby

Redmile

Barnstone

Barkestone

Langar

Plungar

Belvoir
B

Woolsthorpe
by Belvoir

Owthorpe

D
Colston
Bassett

A

Harston

E

Harby

Stathern

Knipton

Kinoulton

Branston

F

Hose

Eaton

Hickling

Long Clawson

Goadby
Marwood

Upper
Broughton
A606

G Nether
Broughton

Waltham
on the
Wolds

Queensway
Old Dalby

Old Dalby

Holwell

Scalford

Wartnaby

Ab Kettleby

Grimston

Saxelbye

H

Asfordby
Hill

Thorpe
Arnold

Asfordby
Valley

Melton
Mowbray

Sysonby

Bottesford church

Naturescape wild flower farm

Belvoir Castle

TOWERS OF POWER

An easy-going metric century taking in each side of the River Trent

———

Located at the point where the Roman Fosse Way and the medieval Great North Road cross the River Trent, Newark — it has long been said — was the 'key to the North'. With all that history, a formidable castle overlooking the bridge and a superb, continental-style market place, it's a good town to explore on foot and to use as a base for cycling forays into the surrounding countryside.

The Trent plain between Newark and the Humber estuary is so flat it can be a disorienting landscape for wayfarers. There are few natural vantage points and no distant hills to help with orientation. In this great expanse of the horizontal, anything vertical takes on a special stature. For centuries the tallest buildings were church spires and windmills. In the mid-twentieth century a third kind of structure appeared to dwarf these ancient landmarks: the power station cooling tower. This ride takes in all three. At 60 miles (just shy of a metric century of 100 km) it's the longest ride in this book but the absence of any real hills makes the going easier. There's also an obvious shortcut that can cut it down it to just under 40 miles if required.

From Newark, National Cycle Route 64 heads north on the eastern bank of the River Trent, along the edge of the RSPB's Langford Lowfields, a wetland nature reserve slowly emerging from a working sand and gravel quarry Ⓐ. Among the habitats are reedbeds, wildflower-rich meadows, areas of thorny scrub and a small mature woodland. NCR 64 picks a way north, avoiding the main roads. The first windmill on the route is at the village of Harby. It was working up until the 1930s, and has now been converted into a five-storey private dwelling. It is best viewed from the driveway off Wigsley Road Ⓑ.

Just past Harby is the trackbed of the old Lincoln to Chesterfield railway. The line once carried holidaymakers to seaside resorts at Cleethorpes and Mablethorpe, and — coming the other way — fragrant high speed 'fish trains' loaded with the catch of the day from Grimsby. Now repurposed for cycling and walking, and part of a long-distance Sustrans route between Clumber Park and Lincoln, the railway line crosses the Trent on the 59-arch Fledborough Viaduct Ⓒ.

In the absence of bridges, the only way to cross the Trent was by ford or by ferry. People have most likely been crossing the river at Laneham since Roman times — there are Roman tiles in the walls of the church. The ferry service ran until 1923, though the Ferryboat Inn remains so named a century later. Until well into the 1960s the riverbank and shingle shore at Laneham

START & FINISH: Newark • DISTANCE: 60 miles / 97km • TOTAL ASCENT: 394m
TERRAIN: Lanes and 7 miles of good gravel cycleways and byways. Moderate.

River Trent

Newark Castle

served as a kind of beach resort for local people. On fine summer weekends many hundreds would come to sunbathe, socialise and cool off in the river. From a few miles downstream of Newark the Trent is tidal; in 2015 a harbour porpoise was spotted swimming here (you can see the footage on YouTube) ⒟.

From Laneham a good gravel track leads to the perimeter fence of the Cottam Power Station and its eight giant cooling towers. Built in the 1960s, at peak flow it would burn 18,300 tons of coal a day, and the cooling towers use evaporation and condensation to cool the superheated steam from the turbines. Cottam's coal plant was closed in 2019 and the towers are now awaiting demolition ⒠.

Writing in 1991, Marina Warner described cooling towers as "outstanding examples of twentieth-century technological resourcefulness".

She went on to argue that "they also symbolise heedless, overflowing consumption with an ironic economy of form. And so, in my eyes they are significant, apt and beautiful monuments of our time." Given their role in man-made climate change, Warner wondered whether the cooling tower "will come to seem a magnificent folly, a modern version of the Aztec temple to the god of the sun." Three decades later, the question is whether any cooling towers will be preserved for future generations to look up at, with a mixture of wonder and remorse?

From Cottam it's a few miles of lanes to the windmill at North Leverton ⒡. Most of Britain's working windmills are of the modern wind turbine variety, generating the low-cost electricity that has put power stations like Cottam out of business. But the windmill at North Leverton is one of a very few left still grinding wheat, as it has done for over 200 years. Near the communications mast at Grove the route reaches its highest point, a dizzying 84 metres above sea level!

Heading south through large arable fields, the lanes are quieter once you're over the A57 at Darlton. Windmills three and four come in close succession at Sutton-on-Trent Ⓖ and Carlton-on-Trent Ⓗ, two towns on the old Great North Road. The most storied of all British roads, it was the main route between England and Scotland since medieval times. Its modern incarnation is the A1 dual carriageway. This is no road for cyclists and necessitates a detour via Norwell and a fifth and final windmill. The riverside pub at North Muskham is a perfect spot for an end of ride drink before the final run in to Newark on the causeway that carries the Great North Road across the flood plain of the Trent. It's a fast road but there's a shared use cycle path. As you arrive in Newark look out for the towering chimneys and storage silos of the British Sugar plant, one of just four locations where sugar beet grown by British farmers is processed into sugar Ⓘ.

PUBS & PIT STOPS

COUNTRY KITCHEN CAFÉ, Mill House, Laneham Road, Newark NG22 0UW (07758 165457) Unfussy café serving cooked breakfasts, cakes and more.

THE BEES' KNEES, Main Street, Laneham DN22 0NA (01777 228090) Best pub en route, serving beer from the Springhead brewery next door. Hearty food.

FERRYBOAT INN, Church Laneham DN22 0NQ (01777 228350) Trad pub near the river. Food served.

TRENTFIELD FARM, Church Laneham, Retford DN22 0NJ (01777 228651) Caravan and motor-home oriented campsite with tent pitches near the river.

THE DELI AT NO. 4, 4 Main St, Sutton on Trent NG23 6PF (01636 823999) Stylish deli selling drinks and snacks as well as meat from local producers.

THE LORD NELSON INN, 35 Main Street, Sutton on Trent, NG23 6PF (01636 821885) Fairly run-of-the-mill pub with rooms for B&B.

THE MUSKHAM FERRY, Ferry Lane, North Muskham NG23 6HB (01636 704943) Popular pub with riverside garden. Pub grub.

BIKE SHOP: Newark Cycles, 53 Balderton Gate, Newark NG24 1UE (01636 612010).

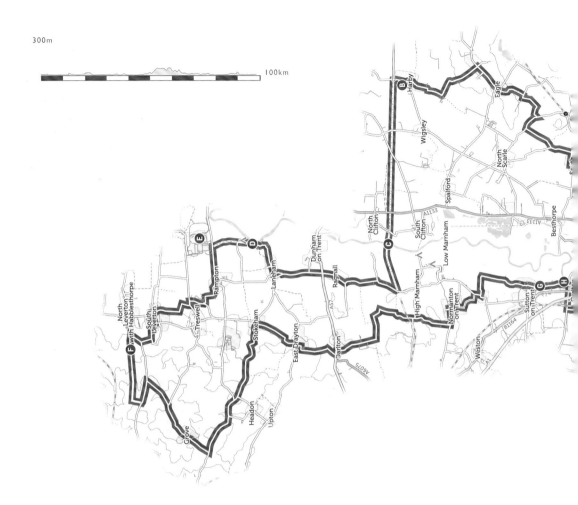

300m

100km

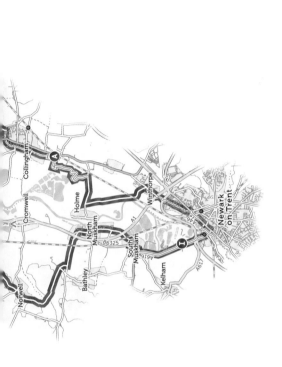

Carlton-on-Trent windmill

Sutton-on-Trent windmill

British Sugar, Newark

North Leverton windmill

No.28

THE WAY THROUGH THE WOODS

A rough-stuff ramble on the forest trails and farm tracks
of Sherwood Forest and the Dukeries

———

The legend of Robin Hood combines the mystery and magic of the forest with the romance of the heroic outlaw. The historical context was the early medieval class conflict between England's Norman rulers and its Anglo-Saxon peasantry. The French-speaking kings declared large swathes of the country as their private hunting ground, and stopped local people from exercising their traditional rights to gather wood, to hunt, and to fence in their crops. Robin Hood emerges as a noble brigand who steals from the rich to give to the poor and resists the tyranny of the powerful. Wise in the ways of the greenwood, Robin and his band of Merry Men roamed the royal forest of Sherwood, which once stretched from Nottingham to Worksop.

Today, only a fraction of the old forest remains, much of it within four large aristocratic estates collectively known as the Dukeries. This ride takes in tracks and bridleways with unpaved surfaces: in summer, many paths will be bone dry, while after a winter of heavy rains the same paths can be muddy.

The ride begins in Creswell and makes straight for Creswell Crags, a limestone ravine east of the town and one the most important archaeological sites in Britain. Around 40-50,000 years ago the gorge, which is dotted with caves and caverns, was inhabited by Neanderthal people, who left behind stone hand-axes and other tools. Later, when a great wall of ice extended from the Arctic to just a few miles north of here, people used the caves as a seasonal base as they hunted wild horses, deer, bison, reindeer, mammoth and woolly rhinos. They were not just hunters but artists: the gorge contains Europe's most northerly cave art, as well as the oldest piece of artwork ever found in Britain, the head of a wild horse engraved on a rib bone, around 12,000 years old. The visitor centre provides information on the geology and archaeology, and can arrange tours of the caves (£) Ⓐ.

Creswell Crags is part of the 15,000-acre Welbeck Estate, owned by the Dukes of Portland. There is only one cycling right of way across the estate, a track through wood and field that can be rough and soft under wheel in places. Passing all the well-kept estate roads and forest tracks with imposing gates and "Private" signs is enough to rekindle the trespassing spirit of Robin Hood. Things are much better in neighbouring Clumber Park, once the country seat of the Dukes of Newcastle but now owned by the National Trust. The big house burned down, but there is a lake, Europe's longest avenue of lime trees Ⓑ, a 4-acre walled kitchen garden Ⓒ and many miles of traffic-free trails that are perfect for children and

---

START & FINISH: Creswell • DISTANCE: 39 miles / 63km • TOTAL ASCENT: 526m
TERRAIN: Half lanes and half unpaved forest tracks and bridleways,
with a few rougher sections that can get muddy after rain. Challenging.

Creswell Crags

novice cyclists. My route follows a trail around the lake to Hardwick, the neo-Elizabethan village built to house estate workers Ⓓ.

Leaving Clumber Park and crossing the A614, woodland gives way to farm fields, on lanes through Bothamsall, then an unpaved farm track towards Walesby. A good bridleway beside the clear waters of the River Maun leads all the way to Ollerton. The old part of the town is handsome red brick, with a large former coaching inn facing the old watermill across the market place and the river running through. The newer part of the town was built around a coal mine sunk in the 1920s, which turned Ollerton into a colliery town. Ollerton was a flashpoint during the miners' strike of 1984-85, probably the most bitter industrial dispute in British history. Rather than a row about

pay, the strike was a reaction to the government's plans to close dozens of collieries it considered to be uneconomic. Nottinghamshire miners tended to be less militant than miners elsewhere and felt their modern, profitable pits were less threatened by closure. Most, though not all, kept working during the strike. This enraged their striking comrades. When Ollerton was picketed by striking miners from South Yorkshire there were running battles in the streets between the police, pickets and miners trying to get to work. The bitter divisions between strikers and 'scabs' continued long after the mine was closed in 1994.

Just beyond Ollerton is Rufford Abbey Country Park, a medieval abbey and landed estate now owned by the local council. Cycling through the grounds is not permitted, which is frustrating. To get from Rufford Mill to the impressive and free-to-visit ruins of Rufford Abbey Ⓔ you must either use the busy A614 (not recommended) or play Robin Hood and take your chances on one of the woodland tracks. The aptly named Vexation Lane leads to a good track beside the razor-wire fencing of the Centre Parcs holiday resort. Except for a short stretch of the B6030 it's all off-road tracks through coniferous plantations of Sherwood Pines, into the heart of Sherwood Forest. Though now less than 5% of its original extent, there still are around a thousand veteran oaks in the area known as the Birklands Ⓕ. The largest and most famous tree is the Major Oak, a mile detour from the route Ⓖ. The biggest oak in Britain is a rather sad sight, supported by metal scaffolding, enclosed by fencing and cut off from the life of the forest.

Quiet farm lanes lead back to Creswell. On the way into the town, look out for the 1890s Arts and Crafts-style 'model village' built for local coal miners and their families Ⓗ. The spacious terraced cottages are built in two circles around a large green. The adjacent village institute included a bar and billiard room, a reading room, a library and lecture theatre, allotments and a cricket ground.

PUBS & PIT STOPS

THE HARLEY CAFE, The Welbeck Estate S80 3LW (01909 478725) Off-route and slightly tricky to reach given the estate's anti-cycling policies, but a great café close to the free-to-visit Harley Gallery and Portland Collection museum.

NATIONAL TRUST CAFÉ, Clumber Park S80 3AZ (01909 544917) Hot drinks, cakes and light lunches with plenty of outside seating.

OLLERTON WATERMILL TEASHOP, Market Place, Ollerton NG22 9AA (01623 822469) Small, highly rated tea rooms and café in the old watermill; booking advised.

HOP POLE HOTEL, Main Street, Ollerton NG22 9AD (07771 555354) Handsome Georgian coaching inn now a pub-hotel-restaurant run by the Samuel Smith brewery.

THE WHITE HART, Market Place, Ollerton NG22 9BL (01623 822410) Traditional Samuel Smith's boozer.

THE MILL CAFÉ AND PIZZA SHED, Rufford Abbey Mill, Rufford Lane NG22 9DF (01623 821338) Elegant Georgian watermill complex with traditional café and pop-up pizza joint.

CAMPING IN THE FOREST, Sherwood Pines, Kings Clipstone, NG21 9JL (01623 572337) Well-equipped Forestry Commission campsite with 150 pitches in 40 acres of woodland.

Plenty of choice in Creswell. Post-ride fish and chips at **THE TRAWLERS CATCH**, 22 Elmton Rd (01909 720868) or **CRESWELL FISH BAR**, 70 Elmton Road (01909 721356). **OURS**, 2 Elmton Road (01909 307976) is a community-oriented pub serving food.

BIKE SHOP and **BIKE HIRE**: Sherwood Pines Cycles, Sherwood Pines Forest Park, Old Clipstone NG21 9JL (01623 822855).

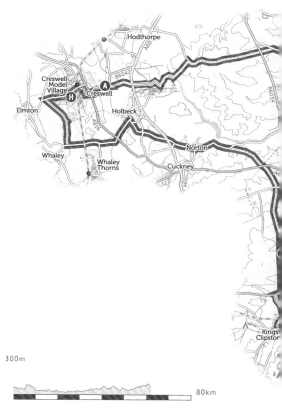

300m

80km

The Major Oak

The Hop Pole Inn, Ollerton

From the magnificent cathedral city to the ancient
ridgeway across the Lincolnshire Wolds

———

While most of Lincolnshire is as flat as a pancake, the rolling hills which extend from Spilsby in the south all the way to the Humber provide some steep gradients and good vantage points for views across the surrounding lowlands. The Wolds are a series of chalk hills, part of the same geological formation as the Yorkshire Wolds, north of the Humber, and the chalk downland that is a defining landscape of southern England, extending from Salisbury Plain to the white cliffs of Dover.

This ride is, in effect, a 20-mile out-and-back from Lincoln to Bardney plus a 40-mile loop from Bardney up to the Wolds. The arterial roads around Lincoln are fast and busy, the cycle infrastructure is patchy but the flat and traffic-free Water Rail Way beside the River Witham is an excellent way out of the city centre, if you're heading east. It continues all the way to Boston, 33 miles away.

The River Witham downstream of Lincoln had one of the heaviest concentrations of abbeys and monasteries in England. The river made for a good trading route for exporting the wool that was the monks' principal source of income. Bardney Abbey, founded in 697 by King Æthelred of Mercia, is the oldest and was the largest Ⓐ. Nothing remains but the faintest traces of its earthworks but, two miles on, at Tupholme, a single stone and brick wall of a smaller abbey is still standing Ⓑ. The monks are long gone; the sheep now use the ruins to shelter from the wind.

In order to keep to quieter lanes, my route bypasses Woodhall Spa, but it's well worth a detour if you've time. The story of how a slice of a leafy Surrey suburb came to this corner of rural Lincolnshire began with the chance discovery of a mineral spring by a landowner who had hoped to find coal. The waters contained a combination of minerals thought to possess curative powers, so a hotel and bath house were soon built. Then, in the 1890s, a whole new town was laid out, combining the novel ideas of the garden city movement with all the trappings of a continental European spa town. Initially wildly successful, after the First World War it entered a long period of decline. The town has seen something of a revival of late, with a popular 1940s-themed festival that draws on the town's association with the World War Two 'Dambusters' air crews, as well as its wealth of period architecture including the unique Kinema in the Woods, built in 1922 and the last cinema in Britain to use back-projection Ⓒ.

From the outskirts of Woodhall Spa, quiet lanes lead to the small market town of Horncastle at the foot of the Wolds. The climb to Fulletby and its trio of hilltop communications masts is where you'll renounce any mistaken belief that

---

START & FINISH: Lincoln • DISTANCE: 60 miles / 96km • TOTAL ASCENT: 625m
TERRAIN: Lanes, B-roads, traffic-free cycleways and 1½ miles of bridleway. Moderate.

Lincoln

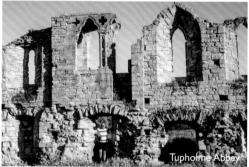
Tupholme Abbey

Lincolnshire is flat. This corner of the Wolds is where the poet Alfred, Lord Tennyson was born and raised. As a young man he wandered the hills by night and by day, reciting poetry as he went. He was known to stop in for a drink at the White Hart Inn in Tetford. Tennyson's poetry was grounded in the landscape and enriched by careful observations of the natural world. He wrote of the "calm and deep peace" he found in the Wolds.

From Tetford it's another short but steep climb onto the Bluestone Heath Road, one of Britain's great ridgeways, running the length of the Wolds from Calceby in the south to Caistor in the north. The short section between Tetford Hill and Red Hill is, to my mind, the most impressive, with a series of panoramic views across the whale-backed hills. The nature reserve on Red Hill, named for the outcrop of red chalk rich in fossils, contains a tiny fragment of the semi-natural grassland that once covered much of the chalk escarpment of the Wolds, before it was 'improved' by ploughing, reseeding and the application of artificial fertilisers Ⓓ. Modern agriculture has increased productivity, but 97% of the wildflower meadows that existed in the 1930s are gone. Species once common now cling on in reserves like this, from the yellow spring flush of cowslips, bird's-foot trefoil and kidney vetch, to the delicate blues and lilacs of harebells and devil's bit scabious, to the deeper pinks and purples of pyramidal orchids and knapweed. The diversity of flora supports a rich ecology of insect and other animals. Look out for marbled white butterflies, fritillaries and six-spot burnet moths.

It is a fast descent from Red Hill to Goulceby where the ride bids farewell to the Wolds, tracking south-west along Green Lane. About half-way between Goulceby and Hemingby, look out for the point where the lane crosses an old Roman road that's now a bridleway Ⓔ. From Hemingby it's a matter of dodging the main roads by sticking to back lanes through Baumber and Gautby and picking up the B1202 back to Bardney. The opening lines of Tennyson's lyrical ballad *The Lady of Shalott* could well have been inspired by the seemingly endless arable landscape: "On either side the river lie / Long fields of barley and of rye, / That clothe the wold and meet the sky." From Bardney the route retraces the Water Rail Way back to Lincoln.

PUBS & PIT STOPS

BARDNEY HERITAGE CENTRE, 123A Station Rd, Bardney LN3 5UF (01526 397299) As well as the small museum there is a café, bike hire and a fish & chip shop.

TEA HOUSE IN THE WOODS, Coronation Rd, Woodhall Spa LN10 6QD (01526 354455) Dating from 1903, and next door to the famous Kinema, it's a popular spot for coffee, cake and light snacks.

THE OLD STABLES, Market Place, Horncastle LN9 5HB (07946 783610) Courtyard café serving good food.

WHITE HART INN, Tetford LN9 6QQ (01507 533255) Village pub that was once Lord Tennyson's local. Pub grub. Rooms available.

LINCOLNSHIRE GLAMPING, Fircombe Hall, Clay Lane, Tetford LN9 6QN (07941 176873) Luxury safari tents high in the Wolds.

THREE HORSESHOES, Shoe Lane, Goulceby LN11 9WA (01507 343909) Outdoorsy pub with seasonal café/bistro and campsite with glamping.

DEAN HOUSE CAMPSITE, Gautby LN9 5RW (07944 247811) Back-to-nature campsite with hot showers, campfires allowed.

BIKE SHOPS: Giant Lincoln Station, 19 St Mary's St, Lincoln LN5 7EW (01522 543781), F & J Cycles, 41F Hungate, Lincoln LN1 1ES (01522 545311).

BIKE HIRE: Bardney Heritage Centre (details above).

Bardney Heritage Centre

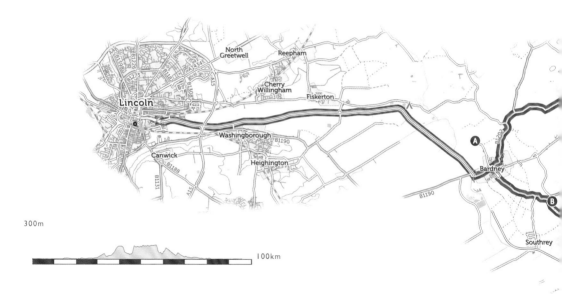

300m

100km

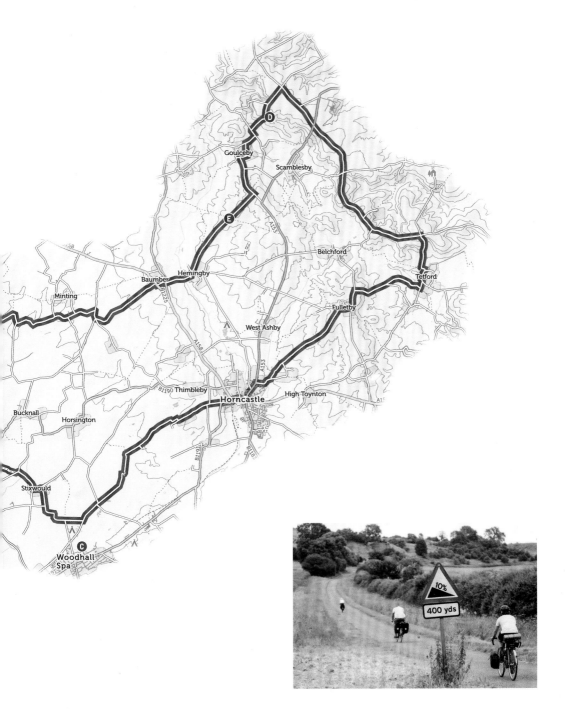

No.30

OUT TO LUNCH

From lovely Louth up into the Wolds
and one of the best pubs in Lincolnshire

———

Louth is an agreeable place, and the people lucky enough to live there seem very happy to do so. The town itself is blessed with some choice Georgian architecture, good independent cafés and shops, and a sense of friendly and easy-going contentedness. All it really lacks is the railway line that was lost back in 1970. Sitting at the foot of the Wolds and on the edge of the North Sea marshes, Louth is also a great base for exploring these two contrasting Lincolnshire landscapes.

This ride heads up over the top of the Wolds to reach, midway, the pretty village of Tealby, whose pub, the Kings Head, dates back to 1367. In a handsome thatch-roofed longhouse with a large, sunny garden, it's the sort of place that defines the ideal of the English country pub. Serving food all day, it makes a perfect half-way stop, though it makes sense to call ahead and book a table.

The route starts out from Louth in the opposite direction to the Wolds, briefly heading towards the coast along the River Lud and its canal twin the Louth Navigation. At Alvingham, it's worth making a very short detour past an 18th century water mill to visit a churchyard which contains, very unusually, not one but two churches Ⓐ. The reason is that, in medieval times, there was a priory here as well: one church was originally a chapel for the nuns, the other served as the parish church for the local population.

What Lincolnshire's fens and marshes lack in hills they make up for in brutal, soul-sapping headwinds. But look east from the road to Yarburgh and you can see all that wind being put to good use. Designed by Sir Norman Foster, the twenty wind turbines on Conisholme Fen supply enough clean, green electricity to power 10,000 homes.

After crossing the A16 at Utterby it's straight up onto the plateau of the Wolds through North Ormsby, another of Lincolnshire's many ancient places. It is mentioned in the Domesday book, Saxon gravestones were found in the churchyard, and beyond the current village there are the earthworks of an abandoned village and former medieval priory. A local curiosity is the White Lady of North Ormsby, a life-size alabaster statue, possibly of Roman origin, which was placed in its current location in 1850 to commemorate the death of a woman in a riding accident Ⓑ. The statue is on private land so to take a closer look you'll need to seek permission from the landowners at Abbey Farm.

At the top of the hill are the remains of RAF Kelstern, a base built during the Second World War. From 1943 to 1945, Lancaster bombers set off from here (and from nearby RAF Binbrook) on night raids over Germany. The blanket bombing of German civilian populations was

---

START & FINISH: Louth • DISTANCE: 43 miles / 70km • TOTAL ASCENT: 593m
TERRAIN: Lanes and 1½ miles of unpaved woodland track. Easy.

not only morally repugnant but strategically counterproductive. Rather than shortening the war, the huge loss of life merely strengthened German resolve to fight to the bitter end. For their part, nearly half of the young airmen who flew the bombers were killed in action, a truly shocking death rate. It is grim chapter in the history of both countries, however you look at it. The airfield has long since reverted to farm fields, though the concrete runways are still just about discernible, and rideable should you feel the urge Ⓒ.

The next few miles take you through the heart of the Wolds, a landscape of flat hills separated by dry river valleys that were carved by snow and glacial meltwaters towards the end of the last Ice

Age. Cycling against the north-south grain of the landscape makes for a sequence of punchy climbs and short descents. Caistor High Street (aka the B1225) is a ridgeway across the Wolds that has been in use at least as far back as Roman times. The route crosses this ancient highway within two miles of Wold Top, which at 168m above sea level is the highest point in Lincolnshire. The spot is marked by a radar station shaped like a giant golf ball. It's a lovely run along Caistor Lane to Tealby, which must rank as one of the prettiest villages in the Wolds or anywhere in Lincolnshire. The Kings Head is a cracking country pub, perfect for a pint and a bite Ⓓ.

South of Tealby, after crossing the A631, is a really good, unsurfaced forest track through

Willingham Woods Ⓔ. From Little London some little-used farm lanes begin the climb back across the Wolds. After recrossing Caistor High Street it's a descent into the glacier-scoured valley of the River Bain. This chalk stream is the principal river of the Wolds, flowing south from Ludford to Horncastle and Coningsby and eventually emptying into the North Sea. There is one last climb up to the Bluestone Heath Road, the ancient ridgeway that runs the length of the Wolds (see Ride No. 29).

The last few miles are a fast freewheeling descent back to Louth. Just on the edge of the town is Hubbard's Hills, a wooded country park set in a steep-sided gorge of the River Lud Ⓕ. Cycling isn't allowed, but anyone can take a walk through the much-loved back garden shared by the lucky people of this most contented of towns.

PUBS & PIT STOPS

AUCTION HOUSE, 1 Cornmarket, Louth LN11 9PY (01507 609128) Stylish café-bar serving great food, from brunch to evening meals.

POCKLINGTON'S BAKERY, 2 Market Place, Louth LN11 9NR (01507 600180). Stock up on Lincolnshire plumbread and other picnic fixings.

THE CHEESE SHOP, 108 Eastgate, Louth LN11 9AA (01507 600407) Cheese heaven, superb savoury pies.

B17 CAFÉ, Back Lane, Binbrook LN8 6DE (07393 339740). Cycle-friendly café serving hot drinks, cakes and cooked breakfasts.

THE KINGS HEAD, 11 Kingsway, Tealby LN8 3YA (01673 838347) Historic thatched country inn with large garden. Good food served all day. Rooms.

A few options in Donington on Bain: THE POST OFFICE, Main Road, LN11 9TJ (01507 343220) is a well-stocked village store; THE BLACK HORSE INN (01507 343640) is a traditional pub with B&B; and T W PRODUCE, Hollengs Lane LN11 9TH is a stall selling local farm produce.

BIKE SHOPS: Louth Cycle Centre, Unit 15, Station Estate, Newbridge Hill, Louth LN11 0JT (01507 607447). Halfords, Unit 1 Fairfield Industrial Estate, Tattershall Way, Louth LN11 0HS (01507 353740).

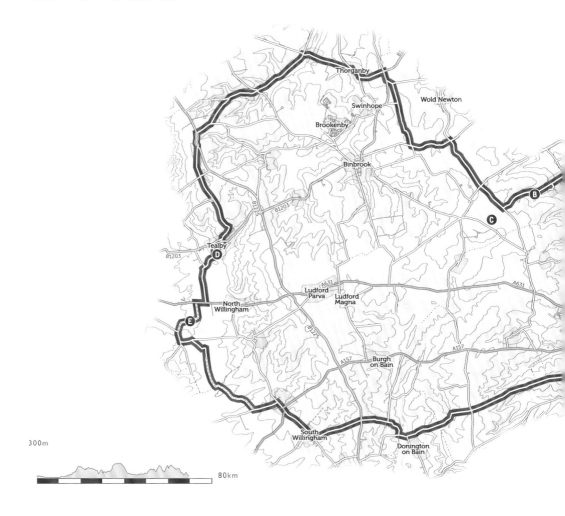

300m

80km

The King's Head, Tealby

ORGANISED
RIDES

No.31

CAT & FIDDLE CHALLENGE

A popular and long-running sportive with a sprinkling of bike racing stardust

———

Cyclesportives come and go, but the Cat & Fiddle Challenge has real staying power. This may be because it was founded by Brian Rourke, a stalwart in the British bike racing scene. A top domestic racing cyclist in the 1960s, Rourke went on to found a company that builds high end bikes for top professionals and discerning amateurs. Custom designed to fit the rider like a well-tailored suit, and skilfully hand-made in Stoke-on-Trent, Rourke lightweight steel bicycles remain among the very best money can buy.

The sportive was first run in 2002 taking in some of Brian Rourke's favourite training roads and over the years has been ridden by stars (and former Rourke customers) like Sean Kelly, Malcolm Elliot, Nicole Cooke and Jason Kenny. It has recently been updated to swap out the busier A-roads for quieter lanes. The organisers say it is now much more of a "riders' route". At 60 miles (96 km) long with 1,300m of climbing the ride requires a decent level of fitness.

The centrepiece of the route is a climb known as the Cat & Fiddle, from Macclesfield into the Peak District. Six miles long and gaining over 300m in elevation, it is one of the longest climbs in Britain and has featured in dozens of bike races including the Tour of Britain. It is an A-road, however, and definitely not a lost lane. The amount of motor traffic can sometimes be off-putting, which is why it makes sense to ride it in a mass participation event. With between 600 and 1,000 riders taking part, drivers get the message to slow down and give plenty of room.

The route also passes local sights including Mow Cop Castle, the astronomical observatory at Jodrell Bank, the Roaches rock formation and Flash, the highest village in England. It is signposted and there are feed stations along the way. The event mostly attracts riders on road bikes but over the years people have completed it on all kinds of bikes, including tandems, mountain bikes and even BMXs. As well as the full distance route there is also a more entry-level route at around 40 miles without the tough climbing into the Peak District. The rides start at Port Vale FC's ground in Burslem, Stoke-on-Trent, just up the road from the Rourke Cycles shop. It's a spacious event HQ with plenty of car parking. Emergency technical assistance is available to all riders from mobile mechanics and there are refreshments at the end of the ride.

Over the years the Cat & Fiddle Challenge has raised over £750,000 for charitable causes. The event currently supports Livability, a UK charity that provides a wide range of care, education and rehabilitation services to over a thousand people living with complex and severe disabilities in order that they can live full and flourishing lives.

Start/finish: Port Vale FC, Burslem, Stoke-on-Trent
Second Sunday in September
£25 early bird, entries on the day accepted
catandfiddlechallenge.co.uk

No.32

TOM SIMPSON RETRO RIDE
AND CYCLING FESTIVAL

Celebrate the life of Nottinghamshire's legendary cycling champion
by riding his home roads at this retro-themed weekender

Tom Simpson was Britain's first international cycling superstar. The son of a coal miner, he grew up in modest surroundings in a Nottinghamshire colliery town. After proving himself on the domestic racing scene, in 1959, aged 21, he moved to France with two bikes and £100 in savings. He went on to win the Tour of Flanders and wore the leader's yellow jersey in the Tour de France where he finished sixth overall. He was the first British rider to win the men's world championship road race, and the first cyclist to win the BBC's Sports Personality of the Year.

Classy on the bike, Simpson cut an entertaining figure off the bike too. Though Simpson's roots were solidly working class, he was often styled as a cartoon English gentleman in a suit and bowler hat, with an umbrella and cup of tea, or clowning about with a ukulele à la George Formby. The French public lapped it up and his sponsors loved the publicity. For all his success and his panache on and off the bike, Simpson is most often remembered for the manner of his death while climbing Mont Ventoux during a baking hot day in the 1967 Tour de France. The amphetamines Simpson had consumed during the race were found to have contributed to his heatstroke, exhaustion and death. The tragedy was a turning point in the sport's relationship with doping.

The Tom Simpson Retro Ride and Cycling Festival is run by Chris Sidwells, a leading cycling writer and huge Simpson fan. The two-day festival celebrates Simpson's life in cycling, and the sheer stylishness of the 'golden era' of road racing, from the beautiful steel racing bicycles to the colourful and iconic cycling jerseys worn by the professional racing teams. It takes place in Simpson's home town of Harworth, in the far north of Nottinghamshire. There are two distances: the 50 km 'Moyenne' route and the 84 km 'Grand'. Though not strictly required to do so, participants are encouraged to ride classic bikes (pre-1987). The event makes it a great excuse to dust down that vintage road bike in the shed, as there's sure to be an appreciative audience. The routes run through quiet countryside on roads where Simpson used to train and race. The terrain is generally flat, with some rolling sections and one steep climb. You can choose which route you want to do, on the day.

What marks the weekend out among bike events is the friendly and informal atmosphere, the sense that it's all being run by enthusiasts. The event HQ includes a mini-festival with exhibitions of classic bikes, and trade stalls. Proceeds from the event go to the Tom Simpson Memorial Fund which helps budding young local racing cyclists.

Start/finish: Harworth and Bircotes Town Hall, Bircotes, Nottinghamshire
Usually held in early September
£30 entry fee for riders; festival is free
tomsimpsonmemorialfund.co.uk

No.33

DANNY MASON

HIGHLANDS CHALLENGE

A friendly and well-organised feast of climbing
in the beautiful hills around Ludlow

———

Many of the best bike events are not just rooted in the history traditions of a particular club, but are the brainchild and lasting legacy of a single, dedicated individual. This is one such event. For almost three decades, the Shropshire Highlands Challenge was run by Danny Mason, who devised the event in the 1990s.

He is something of a legend in Ludlow. A club and racing cyclist all his life, Danny (pictured opposite, top right) served in the Second World War as an 18-year-old member of the Parachute Regiment, and took part in the airborne invasion of Germany. After marrying, he and his wife Jean settled in Shropshire and for a time ran the town's Youth Hostel (sadly now closed) and, later, a shop in the town. They were always generous in sharing their passion for the outdoors, from canoeing to camping, walking and cycling. In 2016, approaching his 90th birthday, Danny stepped down as ride organiser, and passed the baton to Isla Rowntree (founder of Islabikes, based just outside Ludlow).

The event is now organised by the Ludlow Cycling Club, and has been renamed in Danny's honour. The Highlands Challenge remains true to the founder's original vision. There is a new route each year in the hills of Shropshire and adjacent counties, of around 65 miles (close to a metric century), many of them on remote lanes. There is excellent riding in every direction on the dense network of quiet B-roads and country lanes. This gives the organisers plenty of options to devise a new route each year to keep things fresh. In the past decade or so, the routes have tended to make use of the labyrinth of lanes to the west of Ludlow, sometimes crossing over the Welsh border. It is a without question a hilly ride, cramming well over 1,000 vertical metres of climbing, sometimes closer to 2,000m. This makes it a genuine challenge for all but the very strongest and fittest cyclists.

There are up three food stops, with plentiful real food (not energy gels) to see you around the course. As you'd expect of a much-loved event that's run by a team of local volunteers, the overall atmosphere is friendly and relaxed. There are some racing snakes who take it fast, but most people are just there for an enjoyable day out. It's mostly road bikes, but there are always a few people on tourers, hybrids and adventure/gravel bikes. The event pulls a good crowd of up to 500 riders and places fill up fast, so securing a spot well in advance is recommended. At the time of writing, Danny is well into his nineties but still going strong. He was at the finish to welcome riders back from the 2021 edition. All event proceeds go to local charities, such as the Shropshire Wildlife Trust.

Start/finish: Ludlow, Shropshire
Usually held in June
£17.50
shropshirehighlandchallenge.co.uk

BARD'S RIDE

There's something for everyone at this day out in the
North Cotswolds, and all for a good cause

———

Philip Larkin's poem Church Going brilliantly captures the atmosphere of a brief, unplanned stop at a church while out on a bike ride. "Hatless, I take off / My cycle-clips in awkward reverence" he recalls, and goes on to describe the atmosphere of an empty village church, the echoey silence of the place, the smell, and the thoughts that spring to his mind. He recognises the church as "a serious house on serious earth" and admits to a "hunger in himself to be more serious". He wonders about the future and asks, "When churches fall completely out of use / What we shall turn them into?"

One organisation that is determined to avert Larkin's bleak future for churches is the National Churches Trust, whose aim is to "promote and support church buildings of historic, architectural and community value" by making grants for repairs, restorations and other activities. For several decades, the Trust, and its county-level affiliates have raised funds for their work by organising sponsored Ride and Stride days, where participants walk or cycle from church to church, and volunteers provide refreshments and church tours. They are listed on which are listed on the National Churches Trust website (search for 'Ride and Stride').

The Warwickshire and Coventry Churches Trust has expanded its own Ride and Stride day into a larger cycling event. This, the Bard's Ride takes place in the gently rolling Cotswold countryside just south of Stratford-upon-Avon. (It's the law that anything that happens within 20 miles of Stratford must contain an allusion to Shakespeare). The event HQ is in the grounds of Honington Hall, a 17th-century country house just outside Shipston-on-Stour. Such a beautiful and spacious venue makes for a great event.

The full-distance route is 60 miles and keeps to quiet lanes, passing through more than a dozen pretty North Cotswold villages. There is also a 25-mile route, a 10-mile family fun ride and a 6-mile walking route that takes in three local churches, and an ingenious church quiz. The routes are all fully signposted, which makes navigation a breeze. On the longer route there is a water stop, and some churches are open with refreshments. Once back to Honington Hall, there's a finishers' party and a BBQ.

Though only in its first few years, the event has proven popular, with around 150 people taking part. The organisers are keen to grow the event while maintaining its friendly atmosphere and not exceeding the capacity of Honington Hall. It's hoped that numbers will reach 200 or 300, enough to generate a festival atmosphere out on the road.

Honington Hall, nr Shipston-on-Stour, Warwickshire
2nd Saturday of September
£15-20 early bird tickets, £25 on the day
bardsride.co.uk

MERIDEN CYCLISTS' MEMORIAL SERVICE

Continue a long-running tradition of remembrance at the 'centre of England'

The first British soldier to be killed in the First World War was a reconnaissance cyclist. Just 17 years old, Private John Parr's job was to ride ahead of his battalion, scouting the terrain for signs of the enemy. In the next four years nearly a million British people — both military and civilian — were killed in the war, among the 40 million who lost their lives worldwide. The collective outpouring of grief was unprecedented; so too was the resolve to remember. At the initiative of the Cyclists' Touring Club, it was decided to establish a memorial dedicated to cyclists who lost their lives in the war. The chosen location was the village green at Meriden, halfway between Birmingham and Coventry, traditionally regarded as the centre of England (the real centre, according to the cartographers, is 11 miles away at a farm near Fenny Drayton in Leicestershire).

After a national fundraising drive, a 30-foot high granite obelisk was erected on the green, facing Meriden's medieval stone cross. Between ten and twenty thousand cyclists attended the inauguration in 1921, riding from all corners of the country. Though the annual remembrance services were widely supported, by the 1930s there were a few dissenting voices. Foremost among them was William Fitzwater Wray, better known as Kuklos, the leading cycling journalist of the time and member of the socialist Clarion Cycling Club. He wrote a pamphlet in the early 1930s entitled "Mendacious Meriden", in which he argued that nationalism and the sanctification of war was putting Britain on a path towards another major conflict.

Until the mid-2010s, the Meriden Rally was a whole weekend of rides and other events to coincide with the remembrance service. The Rally has fizzled out, but the remembrance service continues under the auspices of the Coventry CTC. The outdoor service consists of hymns, readings and prayers plus a wreath laying ceremony in which members of local cycling clubs and organisations lay their wreaths in turn at the cenotaph. The organisers are keen to involve all faiths, and recognition is made of the sacrifices made by cyclists of all nations, in all conflicts. The Heart of England Cycling Club runs two audax events from Meriden and these are often, though not always, held on the Saturday before the service.

To take part in this long-running cycling tradition, either join with Coventry CTC or another local club that is riding out. Alternatively, devise your own route to Meriden, perhaps starting at Coventry Cathedral, where Basil Spence's remarkable modernist cathedral stands beside the roofless bombed-out remains of the old cathedral, and head out of the city via the War Memorial Park.

Meriden, West Midlands
Usually held in May
Free
coventryctc.org.uk

No.36

FOUR CORNERS AUDAX

A small but perfectly-formed family of audax rides in and around
Staffordshire, Cheshire and the Peak District

Randonneuring, also known as audax, is the branch of organised cycling that's devoted to riding long distances. The challenge is to complete the route within the permitted time. There is no prize for coming first; indeed, those who bring up the rear, using the maximum time allowed, are affectionately known as 'full value riders'. The basic unit of audaxing is 200 km in 14 hours. For most people this is a very long day on the bike. There are shorter distances which are a great way to dip a toe into the world of long-distance cycling. After getting a couple of 100 km audaxes under your belt you may feel ready to step up to 200 km. Who knows where it will lead? There are audaxes at 300 km, 400 km, 600 km and more.

Randonneuring is a brilliant way to discover new parts of the country on a tried-and-tested routes designed by people who know the best roads and the best places to refuel. These are not rides for stopping and sight-seeing. It is a different kind of exploring: you get to see a lot of landscape in a single day and discover how far you can ride a bike. Most events cost just a few pounds to enter and there's a real sense of being part of a collective endeavour. You're on your own, but you're not alone.

Four Corners Audax is the work of audax organiser Shaun Hargreaves and a group of cycling friends. Its events, which currently take place twice a year, are a great way to explore Staffordshire, Cheshire and the southern Peak District. Rides of different distances are run on the same day, with some overlap in the routes and checkpoints.

Shaun's favourite route is his Dambusters 200km, which starts at Werrington village hall, just four miles from Stoke-on-Trent railway station. It's a hilly route that takes in locations linked to the famous 617 Squadron, including Derwent Water where the novel 'bouncing bombs' were tested. The route's little brother is the Dukes and Abbots 100km. The Venetian Nights 200km, from Siddington, near Macclesfield, is a half-and-half mix of the flatlands of the Cheshire Plain with the hills of the Peak District. It is timed to coincide with Matlock's autumn festival of floating illuminations. Refreshments are provided at the beginning and end of all rides, and there are well-chosen cycling-friendly cafés en route. 200 km events feature a mobile food stop where Shaun's helpers offer riders "cake, sarnies, tea, coffee and moral support".

There are more than 500 audax events in Britain every year, so there are plenty to choose from. Mark Rigby runs many of his highly-rated Black Sheep events out of Tewkesbury. Beacon Roads CC in Birmingham also runs a popular series of challenging events heading into Wales and the Marches.

Siddington, Cheshire; Werrington, Staffs
Dates: May and September
£10 for 200 km events / £6 for 100 km events
shaun87356.wixsite.com/fourcornersaudax

Lost Lanes Central
36 Glorious Bike Rides
in Central England

Words and photos:
Jack Thurston

Cover illustrations:
Andrew Pavitt

Design and layout:
Amy Bolt

Editorial:
Michael Lee

Proofreading:
Steve Lockley

Distributed by:
Central Books Ltd
1, Heath Park Industrial Estate,
Freshwater Rd,
Dagenham RM8 1RX
Tel +44 (0)845 458 9911
orders@centralbooks.com

Mapping powered by:

Published by:
Wild Things Publishing Ltd
Freshford, Bath, BA2 7WG
hello@wildthingspublishing.com
www.wildthingspublishing.com

lostlanes.co.uk
Twitter @jackthurston
Instagram: @_lostlanes
#lostlanes
#lostlanescentral

Copyright

Photographs and maps

All photographs © Jack Thurston except p.45 (top) © Karen Roe / CC-BY, p.182 (left) © rattan2011 / CC-BY, p.188 (top left) Peter Appleby / public domain, p.204 (top), p.217 (middle & bottom right) © duncanh1 / CC-BY, p.244 © Wayne Jackson, p.246 © Andy Jones, p.250 (top right & bottom) © James Kerr, p.254 (bottom) © Shaun Hargreaves. Map data © OpenStreetMap, licensed under the Open Database Licence. Additional data from Ordnance Survey, licensed under the Open Government Licence (© Crown copyright and database right 2022).

Acknowledgements

I'm grateful to everyone who joined me on recce rides, modelled for photographs and made researching this book such fun. Thanks to: Harry Adès, Sylvie Adès, Ben Brown, Paul Fletcher, Mark Hudson, Des Riley, Will Linford, Matthew Walters, Carol Parsons and Will Alves (glorydays.cc), Julian Hodgson, Adam, Annie and Bill Hayes, Thom and Trafys Hadfield. Thanks to everyone who shared their local knowledge, in particular Arron Bryan, Richard Fairhurst, Debs Butler, David Cox, Mark Beavan, Richard Parker, Chris Sidwells, Shaun Hargreaves, Sarah Constable, Charles Edwards and Jason Oliver. Thanks to Wayne Jackson, Andy Jones and James Kerr for kind permission to use their photographs.

My thanks, as ever, to Andrew Pavitt for another wonderful cover and to Amy Bolt for her impeccable design work, especially the maps for which my thanks also go to Richard Fairhurst at cycle.travel. I'd like to thank Michael Lee for being such an insightful and supportive editor and Steve Lockley for his eagle eyes. The responsibility for any factual errors is mine. Heartfelt thanks to Daniel and Tania, for believing in Lost Lanes and bringing another book to fruition with all the encouragement and support I could ask for. Finally, my love to Sarah, Lewin and Rosa for making our family life on two wheels so much fun and for not missing me too much while I was away on the road or sleeping in a ditch.

Other books from Wild Things Publishing

Wild Guide Central England	Wild Garden Weekends	Bikepacking
Wild Guide Wales	Wild Swimming Britain	Wild Running
Wild Guide Scotland	Wild Swimming France	Lost Lanes South
Wild Guide Lakes & Dales	Wild Swimming Italy	Lost Lanes Wales
Wild Guide South-West	Wild Swimming Spain	Lost Lanes West
Wild Guide South-East	Wild Swimming Sydney	Lost Lanes North
Wild Guide Scandinavia	Wild Swimming Walks	Scottish Bothy Bible
Wild Guide Portugal	Hidden Beaches Britain	Scottish Bothy Walks